Regency Etiquette:
The Mirror of Graces (1811)

by a Lady of Distinction

∽

ENLARGED EDITION

∽

With Additional Period Illustrations

R.L. Shep
Mendocino

ISBN 0-914046-24-1

Printed in the United States of America

Published by:
R.L. Shep
P.O. Box 668
Mendocino, CA 95460

Distributed by:
R.L. Shep Publications
P.O. Box 2706
Fort Bragg, CA 95437

Library of Congress Cataloging-in-Publication Data

Lady of distinction, 19th cent.
  [Mirror of the graces]
  Regency etiquette : the mirror of graces (1811) / by a Lady of distinction. — Enl. ed., with additional period illustrations.
       p.   cm.
  Originally published: The mirror of the graces. London : B. Crosby, 1811. With additional illustrations.
   ISBN 0-914046-24-1
   1. Etiquette for women—England—History—19th century—Sources.
2. England—Social life and customs—19th century—Sources.
3. Costume—England—History—19th century—Sources.   I. Title.
BJ1876.L33   1997
395.1'44—dc21   97-19223
                                                           CIP

THE

Mirror of the Graces;

OR,

THE ENGLISH LADY'S COSTUME:

Combining and Harmonizing

TASTE AND JUDGMENT, ELEGANCE AND GRACE,
MODESTY, SIMPLICITY, AND ECONOMY,

WITH FASHION IN DRESS;

And adapting the various Articles of Female Embellishments to
different Ages, Forms, and Complexions; to the Seasons
of the Year, Rank, and Situation in Life:

WITH USEFUL ADVICE ON
FEMALE ACCOMPLISHMENTS, POLITENESS,
AND MANNERS;

The Cultivation of the Mind and the Disposition and Carriage of
the Body: offering also the most efficacious Means of preserving

BEAUTY, HEALTH, AND LOVELINESS.

The whole according with
THE GENERAL PRINCIPLES OF NATURE AND RULES OF
PROPRIETY.

BY A LADY OF DISTINCTION,

Who has witnessed and attentively studied what is esteemed truly
graceful and elegant amongst the most refined Nations of Europe.

LONDON:

PRINTED FOR B. CROSBY AND CO.
STATIONERS' COURT, LUDGATE STREET; AND SOLD BY
ALL BOOKSELLERS.

1811.

Publication History

This book was first published in
London in 1811
(of which this is an enlarged
photo-reprint)
subsequently in
New York in 1813
New York in 1815
Edinburgh in 1830
Boston in 1831

J. Swan and Son, Printers, 76, Fleet Street, London

CONTENTS.

CONTENTS.

CHAPTER III.

CHAPTER IV

CHAPTER V.

CHAPTER VI.

CHAPTER VII.

CHAPTER VIII.

CHAPTER IX.

CONTENTS

CHAPTER X.

On the management of the person in dancing, and in the exercise of other female accomplishments.

CHAPTER XI.

Continuation of the same subject.—Demeanour to different ranks—to inferiors, equals, superiors.—Precedence.—Society like the solar system.—Court laws.—Graceful obedience to them.—The influence of women in society.

CHAPTER XII.

Conclusion.—The voice—its modulation.—Speech.—Conversation.—General address to the fair of England.

PREFACE.

THE writer of the following treatise on the art in which consist the strength of BEAUTY, the fascination of ELEGANCE, and the all-conquering power of TASTE, is a LADY who has past several years in an intimate acquaintance with the manners and fashions, not only of the highest rank in this country, but also of most of the foreign courts.

These pages were not intentionally at first written for publication, but originally composed by the desire of some female friends, who live at a remote part of the west of England; and who, aware of her consummate knowledge of the world, and experience in all that is honourable

in the art of *captivation,* had applied to
her for certain directions on the subject.
She indulgently complied with their request, and in the elegant treatise we
now present to our readers, gratified her
friends with as fine a lesson on PERSONAL
and MENTAL accomplishments as could
ever flow from the experienced and delicate pen of a woman of VIRTUE and of
TASTE. They were so delighted with
the useful advice it contained, that they
instantly formed a wish to make it public.
Long was the reluctance of the modest
writer; yet after the solemn promise of
her remaining anonymous, and some irresistible arguments grounded upon the
ultimate and infallible advantage that was
to result from the treatise being printed,
the amiable author yielded at last to their
entreaties, and a few additions, as well
as local alterations, were made by herself
to render it still more suitable to the fair

sex in general. The editor now presents it with confidence to the world, well aware that, while he offers to his fair countrywomen a most skilful and efficient HANDMAID in the decoration of their persons, he accompanies the gift with the presence of a MENTOR, who has as much power to adorn the MIND as to decorate the BODY.

We are told by several ancient historians, that CORNELIA, the venerable mother of the GRACCHI, spent the best part of her time in the education of her children, and spared no care, no attention, no trouble, to render them worthy of herself, the *daughter of* SCIPIO, and of their name. They add, that she was so justly proud of them, that, to a rich Campanian lady, her guest, who with ridiculous complacency and girlish ostentation, exhibited the precious caskets which contained her most valuable jewels, she said, pointing to her own children returning from school, " These are my best ornaments."—That every mother should be enabled to say thus much of her daughter, and that every daughter should strive to become the best jewel of her mother, is what the author seems to have had constantly in view in this little volume.

Her wise and select directions, which would come with an ill grace from the pen of a writer of the opposite sex, are here delivered with that *delicacy* and *confidence* which cannot exist but between *virtuous* women on a subject which concerns them *exclusively*.

At the end of the treatise a few useful *recipes* are added, which may amply and innocently supply the place of cosmetics; which, while they seem to beautify for a day, often render hideous for years. These are efficacious, and have so steadily borne the test of experience, that no lady need fear their application.

THE EDITOR.

Plate 1.

Corbould del.

Hopwood fc.

Morning or Domestic Dresses

Published by B.Crosby & C? Jan.y 1810

Plate 2.

Orbould del.

Hopwood sc

Carriage or Promenade Dresses.

Published by B.Crosby &Cº Jan.1ᵗʰ 1811.

DESCRIPTION OF THE PLATES.

HAVING largely treated, in the following pages, on the different degrees of female attire, as suited to the several orders of the British fair, and endeavoured to instruct them in the requisite art of adapting, appropriating, and combining with utility and effect; having besides shown that taste and elegance are not to be acquired by an exorbitant expenditure; and that grace and beauty are best embellished by modesty, simplicity, prudence and good sense; I have only here to call the attention of my fair friends to the plates which illustrate the present work. These plates contain portraits of the different orders of female costume in Great Britain, selected from sources of the highest class, both as to rank, taste, and fashion: exhibiting a correct and faithful display of that style of female decoration which distinguishes the present era.

The FIRST PLATE represents two ladies in morning or domestic habits. The sitting figure is arrayed in a Flemish jacket and petticoat, of cerulean blue muslin, poplin or Chinese silk, laced up the front of the bust with white silk cord; and the jacket trimmed in narrow vandykes to correspond. An antique frill and cuffs of white lace: a Parisian mob cap of thread lace and beading, ornamented with an appropriate flower in front: half boots of amber colour or buff kid: gloves, a pale tan-colour: an occasional scarf of mohair or Cashmire.

The erect figure is represented in a round high dress of white muslin, ornamented at the feet with a coloured border of laurel leaves, in tambour or embroidery: a square falling collar, trimmed with lace, and Spanish cuffs to correspond: a large emerald or gold brooch confining the dress in the centre of the throat: a rich Turkish cord and tassel ornament the bottom of the waist, and fall in irregular lengths on the left side of the figure. The hair, in dishevelled curls in front, twisted in an Indian knot behind, and confined with bands of twisted silk or muslin, corresponding with the colour of the cord and tassel which embrace the bottom of the waist: Roman shoes, and gloves of the same shade.

The SECOND PLATE represents two figures in carriage or promenade *costumes*. The most prominent appears in a long pelisse, *à la militaire*, which is composed of purple or grey twill sarsnet, or of grass green velvet: an arched collar trimmed with Spanish braiding: the front of the bust ornamented with three rows of silk frogs the colour of the pelisse: arched military cuffs to correspond. The coat confined in the centre of the throat, and at the bottom of the waist, with a brooch and clasps of mother-of-pearl set in gold: a convent mob cap of Paris-net confined under the chin, and ornamented in front with a full flower blended with the curls of the hair; its colours tastefully contrasted with that of the pelisse: half boots or Roman shoes, of purple or buff kid: gloves, a pale lemon colour. The ridicule, when used, should be composed of the same materials as the coat, fixed into a gold lion snap. It is necessary, however, to observe, that this article (though exceedingly convenient, since fashion has excluded the use of the pocket) is considerably on the decline with females of a superior order; but as we hear of no substitute, it can never be completely banished till the fashion of the pocket is revived.

The second figure in the plate appears in a round robe of plain Indian muslin, of a walking length, ornamented at the feet with needlework; stomacher front, and Spanish cuff of the same: a cardinal cloak of coloured twill sarsnet, or green Merino

b

cloth, with high plaited ruff *à la* **Queen Mary**: the
cloak trimmed at the bottom with deep lace, or
entirely round with fur: a helmet cap of white
satin, blended with lace, confined under the chin
with two narrow plaitings of net, and ornamented
in front with a small cluster of Persian roses in
moss: a cameo brooch confines the dress in front
of the bosom, or at the throat; and a clasp of the
same embraces the bottom of the waist: the gloves
are Limerick or French kid.

The THIRD PLATE exhibits two females in
evening dresses. The first figure in a round robe
of white crape, ornamented at the feet with a
flounce of Mechlin lace: an horizontal striped front,
composed of alternate lace and needlework; short
sleeve to correspond: the robe extended over a slip
of gossamer satin, either white, blossom-colour, or
blue: the hair in curls confined, and ornamented
with a bandeau and rose-diadem of pearls, diamonds,
or coloured gems; ear-rings, neck-chain and bracelets to correspond: French watch and chain, with
a cluster of small variegated emblematic seals:
ivory fan, with mount of silver frosted crape:
white satin slippers, with silver clasps or rosettes:
and white gloves of French kid.

The second figure in this plate appears in a robe
of green vellum gauze, or Venetian velvet: the

Plate 3.

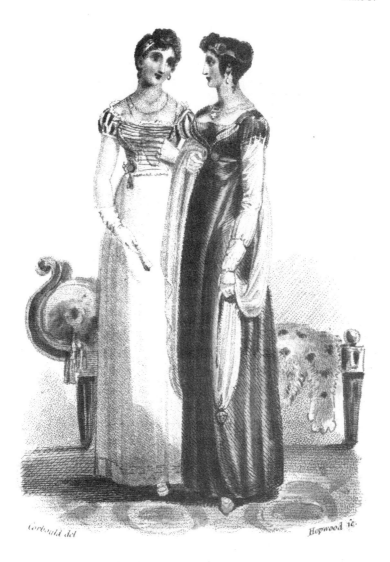

Corbould del

Hopwood sc

Evening Dresses.

Published by B.Crosby & C?.Jan.u.ᵗʰ 1811.

Plate 4.

Corbould del.

Hopwood fc.

Opera or full Dresses

Published by B. Crosby & Cº Jan. 1ᵗʰ 1811.

bosom and sleeves ornamented with alternate folds of white satin, and finished at the feet *en suite:* a full long sleeve of white crape: belt of white satin, confined with a large rose clasp of carved mother-of-pearl and brooch to correspond: union neck-chain of pearl, with Maltese or convent cross, suspended in front of the bosom: a Grecian scarf of silver tissue, or white French silk, the ends gathered into a globe tassel of silver: the hair in irregular curls and ringlets, twisted on one side the head in the eastern style, and ornamented with rolls of silver frosted crape or gauze, finished on the left side with a silver rose: Grecian sandal-slippers appliqued with silver embroidery in front of the foot: gloves of white kid, and fan of carved ivory.

The FOURTH PLATE represents two females in opera or full dress. First figure attired in a round robe, with *demi-train* of pink imperial gauze, worn over a white satin slip, ornamented round the bosom, back, and shoulders, with fine vandyke lace: white satin short sleeves, and appliqued stomacher of white satin, rising above the robe in front of the bust, so as decorously to shade the bosom: a Pomeranian bonnet of white satin, or silver frosted velvet: two white ostrich feathers drooping towards the left side: a diamond or pearl neck-chain, with Carmelite cross: a silver cestus and clasp: a Chinese

scarf of white or fawn-colour silk, with variegated
ends, and narrow corresponding border: white
satin or kid slippers, trimmed with silver fringe:
white gloves of French kid, and fan of spangled
crape.

The second figure in this plate appears in a
Grecian robe of white gossamer satin or sarsnet,
ornamented at the bottom with a deep silver border
in the Egyptian style, and confined up the front,
and across each side the bosom with small turquoise
stone snaps, set in silver filigree: diamond crescent
brooch in front of the bosom: ear-rings, necklace,
and bracelets of brilliants, with turquoise snaps,
and clasps to correspond: the hair in full curls in
front, formed in a helmet crown behind, and ornamented with a wreath of white roses: a large pil-
grim's or Carmelite pelerine of spotted ermine, lined
with blue silk: blue kid slippers, with silver clasps:
gloves of French kid, and fan of carved ivory, with
blue and silver crape mount.

It might be observed that these portraits would
have been more consistent with the rules of
modesty and grace, so much insisted on in the
course of the present work, had the artist more
scrupulously concealed the bosom and shoulders
of the evening and full-dress figures. But the fair
reader must recollect, that these plates are intended

to convey faithful portraits of the reigning fashions of the present times; and I am concerned to add, that in this undue display of the bosom and shoulders, in evening and full-dress, the artist will not be found to have gone beyond the limits of a just representation.

Much is said in the body of this work on the attractive grace and powerful charm of *modesty !* Its advantages are so self-evident, that I am only astonished that policy alone does not prevent the fair fashionable from ever rejecting so becoming and favourable an appendage. " Cheap exhibitions," says an animated writer on this subject, " soon sink into contempt." Unlimited indulgence in any of the pleasures of sense produces satiety, robs imagination of her power and her charms, and destroys the spring of our enjoyments.

> " Learn then, ye fair, to keep the person sacred;
> ———————— like the pure mind,
> Be that array'd in modest dignity:
> Nor e'en its beauties flauntingly expose:—
> Thus may ye keep the heart your charms have won," &c.

And continue unrivalled in the virtues of the heart, and the graces of the mind, as you already are in personal loveliness.

b 3

MIRROR

OF

THE GRACES.

———

PRELIMINARY OBSERVATIONS ON THE SUBJECT.

IN discoursing on the degree of consequence, in the scale of creation, that may be allowed to the human body, two extremes are generally adopted.—Epicureans, for obvious reasons, exalt our corporeal part to the first rank ; and Stoics, by opposite deductions, degrade it to the last. But to neither of these opinions can the writer of these pages concede.

The body is as much a part of the human creature as the mind. It is the medium through which our souls see, feel, and act. By its outward expression of our internal thoughts, we convey to others a sense of our opinions, hopes, fears, and affections : we communicate love, we excite it. We enjoy, not only the pleasures of the senses, but the delights which shoot from mind to mind, in the pressure of a hand, the glance of an eye, the whisper of the heart. Shall we then despise this ready and obedient vehicle of all that passes within the invisible soul? shall we contemn it, as a lump of encumbering clay, as a piece of corruption, fitter for the charnel-house than the bosom of affection?

These ascetic ideas may be consistent with the thankless superstition of the ancient Zenos, or the modern fanatics, who see neither beauty nor joyfulness in the works of the bounteous Lord of Nature; but the rational and fair-judging mind, which acknowledges " use and decency" in all the Creator's works, while it turns from the pagan devotion which the libertine pays to his own body, regards that inferior part of himself with the respect which is due to it in consideration of its Maker and its purpose.

" Reverence thyself!" says the philosopher, not only with relation to the mind which directs, but to the body which executes. God created the body, not only for usefulness, but adorned it with loveliness; and what he has made so pleasing, shall we disesteem and refuse to apply to its admirable destination ?—The very approving and innocent complacency we all feel in the contemplation of beauty, whether it be that of a landscape or of a flower, is a sufficient witness that the pleasure which pervades our hearts at the sight of human charms was planted there by the Divine Framer of all things, as a principle of delight and social attraction. To this end, then, I seek to turn your attention, my fair countrywomen, upon YOURSELVES!—not only to the cultivation of your minds, but to maintain in its intended station, that inferior part of yourselves, which mistaken gravity would, on the one hand, lead you to neglect as altogether worthless; and vanity, on the other, incline you too much to cherish and egregiously to overvalue.

From this you will gather that the *person* of a woman is the primary subject of this discourse.

Mothers perhaps (those estimable mothers, who value the souls as the better parts of their daughters,) may start at such a text. But

I call them to recollect that it is "good all things should be in order!" This is a period when absurdity, bad taste, shamelessness, and self-interest, in the shapes of tire-men and tire-women, have arranged themselves in close siege around the beauty, and even chastity, of your daughters; and to preserve these graces in their original purity, I, a woman of virtue and a Christian, do not think it beneath my dignity to lift my pen.

Dr. Knox will not refuse to be my auxiliary, as a grave auxiliary may be necessary to give consequence to a subject usually deemed so trivial. "Taste requires a congruity between the internal character and the external appearance," says he; "and the imagination will involuntarily form to itself an idea of such a correspondence. First ideas are, in general, of considerable consequence; I should therefore think it wise in the female world, to take care that their *appearance* should not convey a forbidding idea to the most superficial observer."

Another author shall speak for me besides this respected moralist. The very High Priest of the Graces, the discriminating Chesterfield, declared, that " a prepossessing exterior is a perpetual letter of recommendation." To show how different such an exterior is from affectation and extravagance, is one object of these pages; and I hope that my fair and candid readers will, after perusal, lay them down with a conviction that beauty is a blessing, and is to be used with maidenly discretion; that modesty is grace; simplicity, elegance; and consistency, the charm which rivets the attracted heart of well-judging man.

That you have sought my sentiments on these subjects, makes it easier to me to enter into the minute detail I meditate. Indeed, I have ever blamed, as impolitic, the austerity which condemns without distinction any attention to personal appearance. It is surely more reasonable to direct the youthful mind to that medium between negligence and nicety which will preserve the person in health and elegance, than, by leaving a young woman ignorant of the real and supposed advantages of these graces, render her liable to learn the truth in the worst way from strangers, who will either insult her aggravated deformity, or teach her to set off her before-obscured charms with, perhaps, meretricious assistance.

It is unjust and dangerous to hold out false lights to young persons; for, finding that their guides have in one respect designedly led them astray, they may be led likewise to reject as untrue all else they have been taught; and so nothing but disappointment, error, and rebellion can be the consequence.

Let girls, advancing to womanhood, be told the true state of the world with which they are to mingle. Let them know its real opinions on the subjects connected with themselves as women, companions, friends, relatives.— Hide not from them what society thinks and expects on all these matters; but fail not to show them, at the same time, where the fashions of the day would lead them wrong; where the laws of heaven and man's approving (though not always submitting) reason, would keep them aright.

Let religion and morality be the foundation of the female character. The artist may then adorn the structure without any danger to its safety. When a girl is instructed on the great purposes of her existence; that she is an immortal being, as well as a mortal woman; you may, without fearing ill impressions, show her, that as we admire the beauty of the rose, as well as esteem its medicinal power, so her personal charms will be dear in the eyes of him whose heart is occupied by the graces of her, yet more estimable, mind. We may safely teach a well-educated girl that virtue ought to wear an inviting aspect; that it is due to her excellence to decorate her comely apparel.— But we must never cease to remember that it is VIRTUE we seek to adorn. It must not be a merely beautiful form; for that, if it possess not the charm of intelligence, the bond of rational tenderness, is a frame without a soul; a statue, which we look on and admire, pass away and forget it. We must impress upon the yet ingenuous maid, that while beauty attracts, its influence is transient, unless it presents itself as the harbinger of that good-sense and principle which can alone secure the affection of a husband, the esteem of friends, and the respect of the world. Show her that regularity of features and symmetry of form are not essentials in the composition of the woman whom the wise man would select as the partner of his life.—Seek, as an example, some one of your less fair acquaintance, whose sweet disposition, gentle manners, and winning deportment render her the delight of her kindred, the dear solace of her husband. Show your young and lovely pupil what use this amiable woman has made of her few talents ; and then call on her to cultivate her more extraordinary endowments to the glory of her Creator, the honour of her parents, and to the maintenance of her own happiness in both worlds. To do this, requires that her aims should be virtuous, and the means she employs to reach them, of the same nature.

We know, from every record under heaven, from the sacred page, to that of the heathen world, that woman was made to be the helpmate of man : that, by rendering herself pleasing in his sight, she is the assuager of his pains, the solacer of his woe, the sharer of his joys, the chief agent in the communication of his sublunary bliss. To deny this, is to deny even more than the voice of nature; therefore, I shall not stop to answer so wilfully blind an objection.

We have all read in a work, before which kings and sages have bowed, and do now bend the knee, in due humility and deference.—that " a woman's desire is unto her husband !" and for that tender relation, the first on earth, (for, before the bonds of relationship, man and woman became a wedded pair,) woman must leave father and mother, and cleave unto him alone. Hence, I shall not longer beg the question, whether it be not right that a chaste maid should adorn herself with the graces of youth and modesty, and, with a sober reference to the duties of her sex, present herself a candidate for the love and protection of manliness and virtue.

By making the fairness of the body the sign of the mind's purity, man is imperceptibly attracted to the object designed for him by heaven as the partner of his life, the future mother of his children, and the angel which is to accompany him into eternity. Hence, insignifi-

cant as the means may seem, the end is great;
and poor as we may chuse to consider them,
we all feel their effects and enjoy their sweetness.

Having thus explained my subject, my fair
friends will readily perceive that there cannot
be any thing hostile to female delicacy in the
prosecution of my scheme. I give to woman
all her privileges; I allow her the empire of
all her personal charms; I will assist her to
increase their force: but it must be with a
constant reference to their being the ensign of
her more estimable mental attractions. She
must never suppose that, when I insist on
attention to person and manners, I forget
the mind and heart; or when I commend external grace, that I pass unregarded the internal beauty of the virgin soul.

In order to give a regular and perspicuous
elucidation of the several branches of my subject, I shall arrange them under separate
heads. Sometimes I may illustrate by observations drawn from abroad, at other times
by remarks collected at home. Having
been a traveller in my youth, while visiting

foreign courts with my husband, on an errand connected with the general welfare of nations, I could not overlook the influence which the women of every country hold over the morals and happiness of the opposite sex in every rank and degree.

Fine taste in apparel I have ever seen the companion of pure morals, while a licentious style of dress is as certainly the token of the like laxity in manners and conduct. To correct this dangerous fashion, ought to be the study and attempt of every mother, of every daughter, of every woman; and I trust that the veil I would now throw over the bosom of modesty may never again be raised, to sate the voluptuous eye; may never be moved, but by the hand of nuptial happiness, to behold the revealed heart of love and virgin innocence.

GENERAL REMARKS ON THE MANNERS AND FA-
SHIONS OF THE PAST AND PRESENT TIMES.

WHEN Innocence left the world, astonished
man blushed at his own and his partner's
nakedness, and coverings were soon invented. For many an age the twisted foliage of
trees, and the skins of beasts, were the only
garments which clothed our ancestors. Decoration was unknown, excepting the wild flower,
plucked from the luxuriant shrub, the shell
from the beach, or the berry off the tree.—
Nature was then unsophisticated ; and the
lover needed no other attraction to his bride's
embrace, than the peach-bloom on her cheek,
the downcast softness of her consenting eye.

In after times, when Avarice ploughed the
earth and Ambition bestrode it, the gem and
the silken fleece, the various product of the loom
and the Tyrian mystery of dyes, all united to
give embellishment to beauty and splendor to
majesty of mien. But even at that period, when
the east and south laid their decorating riches

at the feet of woman, we see, by the sculpture yet remaining to us, that the dames of
Greece (the then exemplars of the world)
were true to the simple laws of just taste.—
The amply-folding robe, cast round the harmonious form; the modest clasp and zone
on the bosom; the braided hair, or the veiled
head; these were the fashions alike of the
wife of a Phocion and the mistress of an Alci-
biades. A chastened taste ruled at their toilets;
and from that hour to this, the forms and
modes of Greece have been those of the poet,
the sculptor, and the painter.

Rome, queen of the world! the proud dictatress to Athenian and Spartan dames, dis-
dained not to array herself in their dignified
attire; and the statues of her virgins, her
matrons, and her empresses, show, in every
portico of her ancient streets, the graceful
fashions of her Grecian province.

The irruption of the Goths and Vandals
made it needful for women to assume a more
repulsive garb. The flowing robe, the easy
shape, the soft, unfettered hair, gave place to
skirts, shortened for flight or contest,—to the

hardened vest, and head buckled in gold or silver.

Thence, by a natural descent, have we the iron boddice, stiff farthingale, and spiral coiffure of the middle ages. The courts of Charlemagne, of our Edwards, Henries, and Elizabeth, all exhibit the figures of women as if in a state of siege. Such lines of circumvallation and outworks; such impregnable bulwarks of whalebone, wood, and steel; such impassable mazes of gold, silver, silk, and furbelows, met a man's view, that, before he had time to guess it was a woman that he saw, she had passed from his sight; and he only formed a vague wish on the subject, by hearing, from an interested father or brother, that the moving castle was one of the softer sex.

These preposterous fashions disappeared, in England, a short time after the restoration; they had been a little on the wane during the more classic, though distressful, reign of Charles I.; and what the beautiful pencil of Vandyke shows us, in the graceful dress of Lady Carlisle and Sacharissa, was rendered yet more correspondent to the soft undulations of nature, in the garments of the lovely, but frail, beauties of the Second Charles's court. But, as change too often is carried to extremes; in this case, the unzoned taste of the English ladies thought no freedom too free; their vestments were gradually unloosened of the brace, until another touch would have exposed the wearer to no thicker covering than the ambient air.

The matron reign of Anne, in some measure, corrected this indecency. But it was not till the accession of the House of Brunswick that it was finally exploded, and gave way, by degrees, to the ancient mode of female fortification, by introducing the hideous Parisian fashion of hoops, buckram stays, waists to the hips screwed to the circumference of a wasp, brocaded silks stiff with gold, shoes with heels so high as to set the wearer on her toes; and heads, for quantity of false hair, either horse or human, and height to outweigh and perhaps outreach the Tower of Babel! These were the figures which our grandmothers exhibited; nay, such was the appearance I myself made in my early youth; and something like it may yet be seen at a drawing-room, on court-days.

When the arts of sculpture and painting, in their fine specimens from the chisels of Greece and the pencils of Italy, were brought into this country, taste began to mould the dress of our female youth after their more graceful fashion. The health-destroying boddice was laid aside; brocades and whalebone disappear-ed; and the easy shape and flowing drapery again resumed the rights of nature and of grace. The bright hues of auburn, raven, or golden tresses, adorned the head in native simplicity; putting to shame the few powder-ed *toupées*, which yet lingered on the brow of prejudice and deformity.

Thus, for a short time, did the Graces indeed preside at the toilet of British beauty. But a strange caprice seems now to have dislodged these gentle handmaids. We see immodesty on one side, unveiling the too redundant bo-som; on the other, deformity, once more drawing the steeled boddice upon the bruised ribs. Here stands affectation distorting the form into a thousand unnatural shapes; and

there, ill-taste, loading it with grotesque ornaments, gathered (and mingled confusedly)
from Grecian and Roman models, from Egypt,
China, Turkey, and Hindostan.—All nations are
ransacked to equip a modern fine lady; and,
after all, she may perhaps strike a cotemporary *beau* as *a fine lady*, but no son of nature
could, at a glance, possibly find out that she
meant to represent an *elegant woman*.

To impress upon your minds, my fair
friends, that symmetry of figure ought ever to
be accompanied by harmony of dress, and
that there is a certain propriety in habiliment
adapted to form, age, and degree, shall be the
purport of my next observations.

ON THE FEMALE FORM.

To preserve the health of the human form is the first object of consideration. With its health, we necessarily maintain its symmetry and improve its beauty.

The foundation of a just proportion in all its parts must be laid in infancy. A light dress, which gives freedom to the functions of life and action, is the best adapted to permit unobstructed growths; for thence the young fibres, uninterrupted by obstacles of art, will shoot harmoniously into the form which nature drew. The garb of childhood should in all respects be easy ; not to impede its movements by ligatures on the chest, the loins, the legs, or the arms. By this liberty, we shall see the muscles of the limbs gradually assume the fine swell and insertion which only unconstrained exercise can produce : the shape will sway gracefully on the firmly poised waist; the chest will rise in noble and healthy expanse; and the human figure will start forward at the blooming age of youth maturing into the full perfection of unsophisticated nature.

The lovely form of woman, thus educated, or rather, thus left to the true bias of its original mould, puts on a variety of interesting characters. In one youthful figure, we see the lineaments of a wood-nymph; a form slight and elastic in all its parts. The shape, " small by degrees, and beautifully less, from the soft bosom to the slender waist!" a foot, light as that of her whose flying step scarcely brushed the " unbending corn;" and limbs, whose agile grace moved in gay harmony with the turns of her swan-like neck and sparkling eyes.

Another fair one appears with the chastened dignity of a vestal. Her proportions are of a less aërial outline. As she draws near, we perceive that the contour of her figure is on a broader, a less flexible, scale than that of her more ethereal sister. Euphrosyne speaks in the one, Melpomene in the other.

Between these two lie the whole range of female character in form. And in proportion as the figure approaches the one extreme or the other, we call it grave or gay, majestic or graceful. Not but that the same person may, by a happy combination of charms, unite these qualities in different degrees, as we sometimes see graceful majesty and majestic grace. And, certainly, without the commanding figure softens the amplitude of its contour with a gentle elegance, it may possess a sort of regal consequence, but it will be that of a heavy and harsh importance. But, unless the slight and airy form, full of youth and animal spirits, superadds to these attractions the grace of a restraining dignity, her vivacity will be deemed levity, and her activity the romping of a wild hoyden.

Young women must, therefore, when they present themselves to the world, not implicitly fashion their demeanors according to the levelling rules of the generality of school-governesses; but, considering the character of their own figures, allow their deportment, and select their dress, to follow and correct the bias of nature.

There is a class of female contour which bears such faint marks of any positive character, that the best advice I can give to them who have it, is to assume that of the sedate. Such an appearance is unobtrusive; it is amiable, and not only secure from animadversion, but very likely to awaken respect and love.—Indeed, in all cases, a modest reserve is essential to the perfection of feminine attraction. Even heathen fable inculcates this lesson. The God of Love himself once felt the passion he so universally excites. But how? It was not any one of the unzoned nymphs who attended his mother's court that awakened his desire. The gentle influence streamed on him from charms concealed behind a veil! The beauties of Psyche were enveloped in mystery. It was the heavenly cloud of modesty. The sighs of Love could not remove it; even on the nuptial couch it shaded her charms, and she shone the fairer through its snowy medium.

As it has been observed that, during the period of youth, different women wear a variety of characters, such as the gay, the grave, &c. when it is found that even this loveliest season of life places its subjects in varying lights, how necessary does it seem that women should carry this idea yet farther by analogy, and recollect that she has a summer as well as a spring; an autumn, and a winter! As the aspect of the earth alters with the changes of the year, so does the appearance of a woman adapt itself to the time which passes over her. Like a rose in the garden, she buds, she blows, she fades, she dies!

When the freshness of virgin youth vanishes; when Delia passes her teens, and fastly approaches her thirtieth year, she may then consider herself in the noon of her day, but the sun which shines so brightly on her beauties, declines while he displays them, and a few short years, and the jocund step, the airy habit, the sportive manner, all must pass away with the flight of Time. Before this happens, it would be well for her to remember that it is wiser to throw a shadow over her yet-unimpaired charms, than to hold them in the light till they are seen to decay.

From this, my fair friends will easily apprehend that the most beautiful woman is not at forty what she was at twenty, nor at sixty what she was at forty. Each age has an ap-

propriate style of figure and of pleasing; and
it is the business of discernment and taste to
discover and to maintain those advantages in
their due season.

The general characteristics of youth are,
meek dignity, chastened sportiveness, and
gentle seriousness. Middle age has the privilege of preserving, unaltered, the graceful
majesty and tender gravity which may have
marked its earlier years. But the gay manners of the comic muse must, in the advance
of life, be discreetly softened down into little
more than cheerful amenity. Time marches
on, and another change takes place. Amiable
as the former characteristics may be, they
must give way to the sober, the venerable aspect with which age, experience, and "a soul
commercing with the skies," ought to adorn
the silver hairs of the Christian matron.

Nature having maintained a harmony between the figure of woman and her years, it
is decorous that the consistency should extend
to the materials and fashion of her apparel.
For youth to dress like age, is an instance of
bad taste seldom seen. But age affecting the

airy garments of youth, the transparent *dra-pery of Cos*, and the sportiveness of a girl, is an anachronism as frequent as it is ridiculous.

Virgin, bridal Beauty, when she arrays herself with taste, obeys an end of her creation, —that of increasing her charms in the eyes of some virtuous lover, or the husband of her bosom. She is approved. But, when the wrinkled fair, the hoary-headed matron, attempts to equip herself for conquest, to awaken sentiments which, the bloom on her cheek gone, her rouge can never arouse; then, we cannot but deride her folly, or, in pity, counsel her rather to seek for charms, the mental graces of Madame de Sevigné, than the meretricious arts of Ninon de l'Enclos.

But that, in some cases, wrinkles may be long warded off, that auburn locks may preserve a lengthened freshness, is not to be denied; and, where nature prolongs the youth of a Helen or a Sarah, it is not for man to see her otherwise. These are rare instances; and, in the minds of rational women, ought rather to excite wonder, than desire to emulate their extended reign. But what

ought to be, we know is not always adopted.
St. Everemond has told us, that " a woman's
last sighs are for her beauty ;" and what this
wit has advanced, the sex have ever been too
ready to confirm. A strange kind of art, a
sort of sorcery, is prescribed, by tradition and
in books, in the form of cosmetics, &c. to preserve female charms in perpetual youth. But
I fear that, until these compots can be con-
cocted in Medea's caldron, they will never
have any better effect than exercising the
faith and patience of the credulous dupes who
expect to find the *Elixir Vitæ* in any mixture
under heaven.

The rules which I would lay down for the
preservation of the bloom of beauty, during its
natural life, are few, and easy of access. And,
besides having the advantage of speaking from
my own wide and minute observation, I have
the authorities of the most eminent physicians
of every age, to support my argument.

The secret of preserving beauty lies in three
things:—Temperance, Exercise, Cleanliness.
Under these few heads we shall find much
good instruction. *Temperance* includes mo-

deration at table, and in the enjoyment of
what the world calls pleasures. A young
beauty, were she fair as Hebe, and elegant as
the Goddess of Love herself, would soon lose
these charms by a course of inordinate eating,
drinking, and late hours.

I guess that my delicate young readers will
start at this last sentence, and wonder how it
can be that any well-bred woman should
think it possible that pretty ladies could be
guilty of either of the two first-mentioned excesses. But, when I speak of *inordinate* eating, &c. I do not mean feasting like a glutton,
or drinking to intoxication. My objection is
not more against the quantity than the quality
of the dishes which constitute the usual re-
pasts of women of fashion. Their breakfasts
not only set forth tea and coffee, but choco-
late and *hot* bread and butter. Both of these
latter articles, when taken constantly, are
hostile to health and female delicacy. The
heated grease, which is their principal ingre-
dient, deranges the stomach; and, by cre-
ating or increasing bilious disorders, gradually overspreads the before fair skin with

a wan or yellow hue. After this meal, a long and exhausting fast not unfrequently succeeds, from ten in the morning till six or seven in the evening, when dinner is served up; and the half-famished beauty sits down to sate a keen appetite with Cayenne soups, fish, French patées steaming with garlic, roast and boiled meat, game, tarts, sweetmeats, ices, fruit, &c. &c. &c. How must the constitution suffer under the digestion of this *melange!* How does the heated complexion bear witness to the combustion within! And, when we consider that the beverage she takes to dilute this mass of food, and to assuage the consequent fever in her stomach, is not merely water from the spring, but Champagne, Madeira, and other wines, foreign and domestic, you cannot wonder that I should warn the inexperienced creature against intemperance. The superabundance of aliment which she takes in at this time is not only destructive of beauty, but the period of such repletion is full of other dangers. Long fasting wastes the powers of digestion, and weakens the springs of life. In this enfeebled state, at the hour when na-

ture intends we should prepare for general repose, we put our stomach and animal spirits
to extraordinary exertion. Our vital functions are overtasked and overloaded. We
become hectic, (for observation strongly declares, that invalid and delicate persons should
rarely eat solids after three o'clock in the day,
as fever is generally the consequence) and
thus, almost every complaint that distresses
and destroys the human frame, may be engendered. Besides, when we add to this evil
the present mode of bracing the digestive part
of the body, in what is called *long stays*,
to what an extent must reach the baneful effects of a protracted and abundant repast?
Indeed, I am fully persuaded that long fasting,
late dining, and the excessive repletion then
taken into the exhausted stomach, with the
tight pressure of steel and whalebone on the
most susceptible parts of the frame then called
into action; and the midnight, nay, morning
hours, of lingering pleasure,—are the positive
causes of colds taken, bilious fevers, consumptions, and atrophies, By the means enumera-
ted, the firm texture of the constitution is

broken; and the principles of health, being
in a manner decomposed, the finest parts fly
off, and the dregs maintain the poor survivor
of herself, in a sad kind of artificial existence.
Delicate proportion gives place either to mi-
serable leanness or shapeless fat. The once-
fair skin assumes a pallid rigidity or a bloated
redness, which the vain possessor would still
regard as the roses of health and beauty.

To repair these ravages, comes the aid of
padding, to give shape where there is none;
long stays, to compass into form the chaos of
flesh; and paints of all hues, to rectify the
disorder of the complexion. But useless are
these attempts. Where dissipation, disease,
and immoderation, have wrecked the fair vessel of female charms, it is not in the power of
Æsculapius himself to refit the shattered
bark; or of the Syrens, with all their songs
and wiles, to conjure its battered sides from the
rocks, and make it ride the seas in gallant
trim again.

It is with pleasure that I turn from this ruin
of all that is beauteous and lovely, to the
cheering hope of preserving every charm un-

impaired; and by means which the most ingenuous mind need not blush to acknowledge.

The rules, I repeat, are few. Three have clearly been particularised; namely *Temperance:* a well-timed use of the table, and so moderate a pursuit of pleasure, that the midnight ball, assembly, and theatre, shall not occur too often.

My next specific, is that of gentle and daily *Exercise* in the open air. This may be almost always obtained, either on horseback or on foot, in fine weather; and when that is denied, in a carriage. Country air in the fields, or in gardens, when breathed at proper hours, is the finest bracer of the nerves, and the surest brightener of the complexion.— But these hours are neither under the midday sun in summer, when its beams scorch the skin and set the blood in a boil; nor beneath the dews of evening, when the imperceptible damps, saturating the thinly-clad limbs, sends the wanderer home infected with the disease that is to lay her, ere a returning spring, in the silent tomb!—Both these periods are pregnant with danger to delicacy and carelessness.

The morning, about two or three hours after sun-rise, is the most salubrious time for a vigorous walk. But, as the day advances, if you chuse to prolong the sweet enjoyment of the open air, then the thick wood or shady lane will afford refreshing shelter from the too-intense heat of the sun.—In short, the morning and evening dew, and the unrepelled blaze of a summer noon, must alike be ever avoided as the enemies of health and beauty.

Cleanliness, my next recipe, (and which is, like the others, applicable to all ages,) is of most powerful efficacy. It maintains the limbs in their pliancy; the skin in its softness; the complexion in its lustre; the eyes in their brightness; the teeth in their purity; and the constitution in its fairest vigour.

The frequent use of tepid baths is not more grateful to the sense than it is salutary to the health, and to beauty. By such ablution, all accidental corporeal impurities are thrown off; cutaneous obstructions removed; and while the surface of the body is preserved in

its original brightness, many threatening disorders are put to the rout.   Colds in the
young, and rheumatic and paralytic affections
in the old, are all dispersed by this simple
and delightful antidote.   By such means do
the women of the East render their skins
softer than that of the tenderest babes in this
climate; and by such means is that health
preserved which, otherwise, the sedentary confinement of their lives must destroy.

This delightful and delicate oriental fashion is now, I am happy to say, embraced
almost all over the Continent.   From the
Villas of Italy, to the Chateaux of France;
from the Castles of Germany, to the Palaces
of Muscovy; we may every where find the
marble bath under the vaulted portico or the
sheltering shade.   Every house of every
nobleman or gentleman, in every nation under
the sun, excepting Britain, possesses one of
these genial friends to cleanliness and comfort.   The generality of English ladies seem
to be ignorant of the use of any bath larger
than a wash-hand bason.   This is the more
extraordinary to me, when I contemplate the

changeable temperature of the climate, and
consider the corresponding alterations in the
bodily feelings of the people. By abruptly
checking the secretions, it produces those
chronic and cutaneous diseases so peculiar to
our nation, and so heavy a cause of complaint.

This very circumstance renders baths more
necessary in England than any where else;
for as this is the climate most subject to sudden heats and colds, rains and fogs, tepid im-
mersion is the only sovereign remedy against
their usual morbific effects. Indeed, so impressed am I with the consequence of their
regimen, that I strongly recommend to every
lady to make a bath as indispensable an article in her house as a looking-glass.

THE SAME SUBJECT, OF FEMALE BEAUTY, MORE EXPLICITY CONSIDERED.

So far, my fair friends, I have thrown together my sentiments on the aggregate of the
female form; I shall now descend to particulars, and leave it to your judgments to
adopt my suggestions according to the correspondence with your different characters.

The preservation of an agreeable complexion (which always presupposes health,) is
not the most insignificant of exterior charms.
Though we yield due admiration to regularity
of features (the Grecian contour being usually
so called) yet when we consider them merely
in the outline, our pleasure can go no farther
than that of a cold critic, who regards the
finely-proportioned lineaments of life as he
would those of a statue. It is complexion
that lends animation to a picture; it is
complexion that gives spirit to the human
countenance. Even the language of the eyes
loses half its eloquence, if they speak from the
obscurity of an inexpressive skin. The life-

blood in the mantling cheek ; the ever-varying hues of nature glowing in the face, " as
if her very body thought;" these are alike
the ensigns of beauty and the heralds of the
mind ; and the effect is, an impression of
loveliness, an attraction, which fills the beholder with answering animation and the
liveliest delight.

As a Juno-featured maid with a dull skin,
by most people, will only be coldly pro-
nounced *critically* handsome ; so a young
woman with very indifferent features, but a
fine complexion, will, from ten persons out
of twelve, receive spontaneous and warm admiration.

This experience (when once we admit the
proposition that it is *right* to keep the casket
bright which contains so precious a gem as
the soul) must induce us to take precautions
against the injuries continually threatening
the tender surface of the skin. It may be
next to an impossibility, to change the colour
of an eye, to alter the form of the nose, or
the turn of the mouth; but, though heaven
has given us a complexion which vies with

the flowers of the field, we yet have it in our power to render it dingy by neglect, coarse through intemperance, and sallow by dissipation.

Such excesses must therefore be avoided; for, though there may be a something in the pallid cheek which excites interest, yet, without a certain appearance of health, there can never be an impression of loveliness. A fine, clear skin, gives an assurance of the inherent residence of three admirable graces to beauty; Wholesomeness, Neatness, and Cheerfulness.—Every fair means ought to be sought to maintain these vouchers, for not only health of body, but health of mind.

I have already given some hints to this purpose; at least as far as relates to the purity of the alimentary springs of sublunary life : those which are in the heart, and point through time into eternity, must not be less observed; for, unless its thoughts are kept in corresponding order and the passions held in peace, all prescriptions will be vain to keep those boiling fluids in check which, in spite

of Roman fard and balm of Mecca, will
spread themselves over the skin, and there
show an outward and visible sign of the
malignant spirit within. Independent of
these intellectual causes of corporeal defects,
disorders of the skin, arising from accidental
circumstances, are more frequent in this
country than in any other; and the fashions
of the day are still more inimical to the complexion of its inhabitants, than the climate.
The frequent and sudden changes from heat
to cold, by abruptly exciting or repressing
the regular secretions of the skin, roughen its
texture, injure its hue, and often deform it with
unseemly, though transitory, eruptions. All
this is increased by the habit ladies have of
exposing themselves unveiled, and frequently
without bonnets, in the open air. The head
and face have then no defence against the at-
tacks of the surrounding atmosphere, and the
effects are obvious. The barouche, for this reason, and the more consequential one of subjecting its inmates to dangerous chills, is a fatal
addition to the variety of English equipages.
Our autumnal evenings, with this carriage and

our gossamer apparel, have already sent many
of my young female acquaintance to untimely
graves.

To remedy these evils, I would strenuously
recommend, for health's sake, as well as for
beauty, that no lady should make one in any
riding, airing, or walking party, without putting on her head something capable of afford-
ing both shelter and warmth. Shakspeare, the
poet of the finest taste in female charms,
makes Viola regret having been obliged to
" throw her sun-expelling mask away !"
Such a defence I do not pretend to recommend ; but I consider a veil a useful as
well as elegant part of dress; it can be
worn to suit any situation; open or close,
just as the heat or cold may render it necessary.

The custom which some ladies have, when
warm, of powdering their faces, washing
them with cold water, or throwing off their
bonnets, that they may cool the faster, are
all very destructive habits. Each of them is
sufficient (when it meets with any predispo-
sition in the blood) to spread a surfeit over

the skin, and make a once beautiful face, hideous for ever.

The person, when over-heated, should always be allowed to cool gradually, and of itself, without any more violent assistant than, perhaps, the gentle undulation of the neighbouring air by a fan. Streams of wind from opened doors and windows, or what is called *a thorough air*, are all bad and highly dangerous applications. These impatient remedies for heat are often resorted to in balls and crowded assemblies; and as frequently as they are used, we hear of sore-throats, coughs, and fevers. While it is the fashion to fill a drawing-room like a theatre, similar means ought to be adopted to prevent the ill effects of the consequent corrupted atmosphere, and the temptation to seek relief by dangerous resources. Instead of the open balcony and yawning door, we should see ventilators in every window; and thus feel a constant succession of pure and temperate air.

Excessive heat, as well as excessive cold, is apt to cause distempers of the skin; and, as the fine lady, by her strange habits, is as prone to such changes as the desert-wandering gipsy, it is requisite that she should be particularly careful to correct the deforming consequences of her fashionable exposures. For her usual ablution, night and morning, nothing is so fine an emolient for any rigidity or disease of the face, as a wash of French or white brandy, and rose-water; the spirit making only one-third of the mixture. The brandy keeps up that gentle action of the skin which is necessary to the healthy appearance of its parts. It also cleanses the surface. The rose-water corrects the drying property of the spirit, leaving the skin in a natural, soft, and flexible state. Where white or French brandy cannot be obtained, half the quantity of spirits of wine will tolerably supply its place.

The eloquent effect of complexion will, I hope, my fair friends, obtain your pardon for my having confined your attention so long upon what is generally thought (though in contradiction to what is felt) a trifling feature, if so I may be allowed to name it.

I am aware of your expectations, that I

would give the precedence, in this dissertation, to the eye. I subscribe to its super-eminent dignity; for none can deny that it is regarded by all nations as the faithful interpreter of the mind, as the window of the soul, the index in which we read each varied emotion of the heart. But, how increased an expression does this intelligent feature convey, when aided by the glowing tints of an eloquent complexion! Indeed, it is the happy coincidence of the eye and the complexion which forms the strongest point of what the French call *contenance*.

The animated changes of sensibility are no where more apparent than in the transparent surface of a clear skin. Who has not perceived, and admired, the rising blush of modesty enrich the cheek of a lovely girl, and, in the sweet effusion, most gratefully discern the true witness of the purity within? Who has not been sensible to the sudden glow on the face, which announces, ere the lips open, or the eye sparkles, the approach of some beloved object? Nay, will not even the sound of his name paint the blooming cheek with deeper roses?

Shall we reverse the picture? I have shown how the soul proclaims her joy through its wondrous medium; shall she speak her sorrows too? Then let us call to mind, who have beheld the deadly paleness of her who learns the unexpected destruction of her dearest possessions! Perhaps a husband, a lover, or a brother, mingled with the slain, or fallen, untimely by some dreadful accident. We see the darkened, stagnant shade which denotes the despair-stricken soul. We behold the livid hues of approaching phrenzy, or the blacker stain of settled melancholy! Heloïsa's face is paler than the marble she kneels upon. In all cases the mind shines through the body; and, according as the medium is dense or transparent, so the light within seems dull or clear.

Advocate as I am for a fine complexion, you must perceive that it is for the *real*, not the *spurious*. The foundation of my argument, *the skin's power of expression*, would be entirely lost, were I to tolerate that fictitious, that dead beauty which is composed of white paints and enamelling. In the first place, as all applications of this kind are as a mask on the skin, they can never, but at a distant glance, impose for a moment on a discerning eye. But why should I say a *discerning eye?* No eye that is of the commonest apprehension can look on a face bedaubed with white paint, pearl powder, or enamel, and be deceived for a minute into a belief that so inanimate a " whited wall" is the human skin. No flush of pleasure, no shudder of pain, no thrilling of hope, can be descried beneath the encrusted mould; all that passes within is concealed behind the mummy surface. Perhaps the painted creature may be admired by an artist as a well-executed picture; but no man will seriously consider her as a handsome woman.

White painting is, therefore, an ineffectual, as well as dangerous practice. The proposed end is not obtained; and, as poison lurks under every layer, the constitution wanes in alarming proportion as the supposed charms increase.

What is said against white paint, does not oppose, with the same force, the use of red. Merely rouging leaves three parts of the face and the whole of the neck and arms to their natural hues. Hence the language of the heart, expressed by the general com‑plexion, is not yet entirely obstructed. Be‑sides, while *all* white paints are ruinous to health, (occasioning paralytic affections and premature death) there are some red paints which may be used with perfect safety.

A little vegetable rouge tinging the cheek of a delicate woman, who, from ill-health or an anxious mind, loses her roses, may be ex‑cusable; and so transparent is the texture of such rouge, (when unadulterated with lead) that when the blood does mount to the face, it speaks through the slight covering, and en‑hances the fading bloom. But, though the occasional use of rouge may be tolerated, yet, my fair friends must understand that it is only *tolerated*. Good sense must so preside to its application, that its tint on the cheek may always be fainter than what nature's pallet would have painted. A violently rouged wo-

man is one of the most disgusting objects to
the eye. The excessive red on the face gives a
coarseness to every feature, and a general
fierceness to the countenance, which trans-
forms the elegant lady of fashion into a vulgar
harridan.

While I recommend that the rouge, we
sparingly permit, should be laid on with delicacy, my readers must not suppose that I in-
tend such advice as a means of making the art a
deception. It seems to me so slight and so innocent an apparel of the face, (a kind of decent
veil thrown over the cheek, rendered too eloquent of grief by the pallidness of secret sor-
row) that I cannot see any shame in the most
ingenuous female acknowledging that she occasionally rouges. It is often, like a cheerful
smile on the face of an invalid, put on to give
comfort to an anxious friend.

That our applications to this restorer of our
usual looks should not feed, like a worm, on the
bud it affects to brighten, no rouge must ever
be admitted that is impregnated with even
the smallest particle of ceruse. It is the lead
which is the poison of white paint; and its

mixture with the red would render that equally
noxious.

There are various ways of putting on rouge.
Frenchwomen, in general, and those who imitate them, daub it on from the bottom of the
side of the face up to the very eye, even till it
meets the lower eye-lash, and creeps all over
the temples. This is an hideous practice. It
is obvious that it must produce deformity instead of beauty, and, as I said before, would
metamorphose the gentlest-looking fair Herse
into a fierce Medusa.

For Brunettes, a slight touch of simple carmine on the cheek, in its dry powder state, is
amply sufficient. Taste will teach the hand to
soften the colour by due degrees, till it almost
imperceptibly blends with the natural hue of
the skin. For fairer complexions, letting
down the vivid red of the carmine with a mixture of fine hair-powder, till it suits the general appearance of the skin, will have the
desired effect.

The article of rouge, on the grounds I have
mentioned, is the only species of positive art a
woman of integrity or of delicacy can permit

herself to use with her face. Her motives for
imitating the bloom of health, may be of the
most honourable nature, and she can with
candour avow them. On the reverse, nothing
but selfish vanity, and falsehood of mind,
could prevail on a woman to enamel her skin
with white paints, to lacker her lips with vermilion, to draw the meandering vein through
the fictitious alabaster with as fictitious a
dye.

Penciling eye-brows, staining them, &c.
are too clumsy tricks of attempted deception,
for any other emotion to be excited in the
mind of the beholder, than contempt for the
bad taste and wilful blindness which could ever
deem them passable for a moment.   There is
a lovely harmony in nature's tints, which we
seldom attain by our added chromatics. The
exquisitely fair complexion is generally accompanied with blue eyes, light hair, and light
eye-brows and lashes. So far all is right.
The delicacy of one feature is preserved in
effect and beauty, by the corresponding softness of the other. A young creature, so

formed, appears to the eye of taste like the
azure heavens, seen through the fleecy clouds,
on which the brightness of day delights to
dwell. But take this fair image of the celestial regions, draw a black line over her softly-
tinctured eyes, stain their beamy fringes with
a sombre hue, and, what do you produce?
Certainly a fair face with *dark* eye-brows!
But that feature, which is an embellishment to
a brunette, when seen on the forehead of the
fair beauty, becomes, if not an absolute deformity, so great a drawback from her perfections, that the harmony is gone; and, as a
proof, a painter would immediately turn from
the change with disgust.

Nature, in almost every case, is our best
guide. Hence the native colour of our own
hair is in general better adapted to our complexions than a wig of a contrary hue. A
thing may be beautiful in itself, which, with
certain combinations, may be rendered hideous. For instance, a golden-tressed wig on
the head of a brown woman, makes both ridiculous. By the same rule, all fantastic tricks

played with the mouth or eyes, or motions of the head, are absurd and ruinous to beauty. They are solicisms in the works of nature.

In Turkey, it happened to be the taste of one of its great monarchs, to esteem large and dark-lashed eyes as the most lovely. From that time all the fair slaves of that voluptuous region, when nature has not bestowed " the wild stag-eye in sable ringlets rolling," supply the deficiency with circles of antimony; and so, instead of a real charm, they impart a strange artificial ghastliness to their appearance.

Our countrywomen, in like manner, when a celebrated *Belle* came under the pencil of Peter Lely, who exhibited to her emulative rivals the sweet peculiarities of her long and languishing eye; they must needs all have the same; and not a lady could appear in public, be her visual orbs large or small, bright or dull, but she must affect the soft sleepiness, the tender and slowly-moving roll of her subduing exemplar. But though Sir Peter's gallant pencil deigned to compliment his numerous sitters by drowning their strained aspects after the model of the peerless *Belle* ; yet, in place of the nature-stamped look of modest languishment, he could not but often recognise the disgraceful leer and hideous squint. Let every woman be content to leave her eyes as she found them, and to make that use of them which was their design. They were intended to see with, and artlessly express the feelings of a chaste and benevolent heart. Let them speak this unsophisticated language, and beauty will beam from the orb which affectation would have rendered odious.

Analogy of reasoning will bring forward similar remarks with regard to the movements of the mouth, which many ladies use, not to speak with, or to admit food, but to show dimples and display white teeth. Wherever a desire for exhibition is discovered, a disposition to disapprove and ridicule arises in the spectator. The pretensions of the vain are a sort of assumption over others, which arms the whole world against them.

GENERAL THOUGHTS ON DRESS AND PERSONAL DECORATION.

EVERY person of just observation, who looks back on the fashions of our immediate ancestors, and compares their style of dress with that of the present times, will not hesitate to acknowledge the evident improvement in ease and gracefulness. When I say this, I mean to eulogize the taste which yet prevails with persons of real judgment, to maintain the *ease and gracefulness* of our assumed Grecian mode, against a new race of stay-makers, corset-inventors, &c. who have just armed themselves with whalebone, steel, and buckram, to the utter destruction of all the naturally-elegant shapes which fall into their hands.

Just before this attempted counter-revolution in the world of fashion, we found that our *Belles* had gradually exploded the stiffness and formality which distinguished the brocaded dame of 1700, from the lawn-robed fair of the nineteenth century. In former ages it seemed requisite that every lady should cut out her garments by a certain erected standard. All seemed in a livery. One mode for gown, cap, and hat prevailed ; and though the materials might be more costly in one than another, the outline was the same ; and thus peculiar taste and fine form were lost in the general prescription of one reigning costume.

But in our days, an English woman has the extensive privilege of arraying herself in whatever garb may best suit her figure or her fancy. The fashions of every nation and of every era are open to her choice. One day she may appear as the Egyptian Cleopatra, then a Grecian Helen ; next morning the Roman Cornelia ; or, if these styles be too august for her taste, there are Sylphs, Goddesses, Nymphs of every region, in earth or air, ready to lend her their wardrobe. In short, no land or age is permitted to withhold its costume from the adoption of an English woman of fashion.

With such a variety to chuse from, she has no excuse, if she unite not the excellencies of them all. It was so that the sculptor of Paphos formed the " beauteous statue that enchanted the world." And in like manner female taste accomplishes its object. A judicious dresser will select from each mode that which is most distinguishable for utility and grace, and combining, adopt them to advantage. This is the art which every woman, who casts a thought on these subjects, ought to endeavour to attain.

Elegant dressing is not found in expense; money without judgment may load, but never can adorn. You may show profusion without grace: you may cover a neck with pearls, a head with jewels, hands and arms with rings, bracelets and trinkets, and yet produce no effect, but having emptied some merchant's counter upon your person. The best chosen dress is that which so harmonizes with the figure as to make the raiment pass unobserved. The result of the finest toilet should be an *elegant woman,* not an elegantly-dressed woman. Where a perfect whole is intended, it is a sign of defect in the execution when the details first present themselves to observation.

In short, the secret of dressing lies in simpli-

city, and a certain adaption to your figure,
your rank, your circumstances. To dress
well on these principles, (and they are the
only just ones) does not require that extravagant attention to so minor an object, as is
usually exhibited by persons who make the
toilet a study. When lad:es place the spell of
their attraction in their clothes, we generally
see them arrayed in robes of a thousand makes
and dyes, and curiously constructed of materials brought from heaven knows where.
Thus much time, thought, and wealth are
wasted on a comparatively worthless object.
To lavish many of the precious hours of life
in the invention and arrangement of dress, is
as criminal an offence, as to exhaust the
finances of your husband or parents by a
thriftless expenditure on its component parts.

The taste I wish to inculcate, is that nicely-
poised estimation of things, which shows it
" worth our while to do *well,* what it is ever
worth our while *to do.*" This disposition
originates in a correct and delicate mind, and
forms a judgment which makes elegance inseparable from propriety ; and extending

itself from great objects to small, reaches the most apparently insignificant; and thus, even in the change of the morning and evening attire, displays to the considerate observer a very intelligible index of the wearer's well-regulated mind.

" Show me a lady's dressing-room," says a certain writer, " and I will tell you what manner of woman she is." Chesterfield, also, is of opinion, that a sympathy goes through every action of our lives; he declares, that he could not help conceiving some idea of people's sense and character, from the dress in which they appeared when introduced to him. He was so great an advocate for pleasing externals, that he often said, he would rather see a young person too much, than too little dressed, excess, on the foppish side, wearing off with time and reflection; but if a youth be negligent at twenty, it is probable he will be a sloven at forty, and disgustingly dirty at fifty. However this may be with the other sex, I beg leave to observe, that I never yet met with a woman whose general style of dress was chaste, elegant, and appropriate, that I did not find, on further acquaintance, to be in disposition and mind, an object to admire and love.

This correspondence between the thoughts and the raiment being established, what was before insignificant, becomes of consequence; and, being rightly understood, good sense will be as careful not to disparage her discretion, by extravagant dress, as she would to evince a sordid mind, by dirt and rags.

I think I see you, my friends, smile, incredulous, at the last sentence. What gentlewoman, you exclaim, who is above the most abject pecuniary embarrassments, can ever have a chance of being so appareled ? A desire of singularity is a sufficient answer. There are a race of women, who, priding themselves on their superior rank, or wealth, or talents, affect to despise what they deem the adventitious aids of dress. Their appearances, in consequence, are frequently as ridiculous as disgusting. When this folly is seen in female authors, or, what is much the same thing, ladies professing a particularly literary taste, we can at once trace its motive. A conceited negligence of outward attractions; and a determination to raise themselves in the opinions of men, by displaying a contempt for what they deem the vain occupations of meaner souls. Wishing to be thought superior to founding any regard on external ornament, they forget external decency; and by slatternness and affectation, render, what is called a learned woman, a kind of scare-crow to her own sex, and a laughing-stock to the other. This error is not so common now with bookish ladies, as it was in the beginning of the last century. Then our sex did, indeed, show that " a little learning is a dangerous thing." They did not imbibe sufficient to imbue them with a sense of its real properties, to show them causes and effects, to make them understand themselves, and close the book in humility. They, poor short-sighted creatures! exchanged the innocent ignorance of Eve, for the empoisoned apple, which, under the cheat of displaying knowledge, fills the eater with a vain self-conceit, while it more openly exposes her mental nakedness to every eye.

The absurdity of their deductions is so obvious, that one wonders how any woman could fall into such an error. Who among them but would think it the height of folly to place over the door of a Museum, to which the proprietor wished to attract visitors, the effigy of a monster so disgusting, as to deter men from entering to see, what might otherwise have afforded them much pleasure? Such effigies might the slip-shod muses of the days of Anne have given of themselves; but most of the modern female votaries of Minerva, aware of the advantages of a prepossessing appearance, mingle with their incense to the Goddess, a few flowers to the Paphian Graces; and that they gain by the devotion, none who have been admitted to the acquaintance of our British Sapphos and Corinnas, can deny.

There is another class of persons who neglect their exterior on account of the consequence they derive from their rank; but instances on such a plea are few in comparison with the insolent slovenliness of the opposite sex, when, springing from the lower degrees

in society, they amass or acquire large fortunes. They aim at notoriety; and common
means, such as expense and show, not raising
them into an *eclat* beyond their equally rich
cotemporaries, ambition leads them to seek
notice by the assumption of a garb of almost
pauper negligence. I remember, some years
since, when on a visit at a large sea-port
town in the north of England, to have been
attracted by seeing at the door of a handsome
house, in one of the principal streets, an elegant modern chariot. I stopped, and, to my
surprise, saw step into it, an old man, of the
meanest and most dirty appearance. A few
days afterwards, while viewing the docks with
a gentleman, who was an inhabitant of the
place, I observed the same wretched-looking
person conversing familiarly with a man of
the first consequence in the town. I enquired
of my friend the name and business of the
shabby old fellow, and received the following brief answer.

He had been taken, when a boy, from very
indigent parents, residing in a northern village; and being a smart lad, was employed

in the drudgery of a banking-house, belonging
to his benefactors. By assiduous application,
and a deep cunning (aided by what is vul-
garly called *good luck)* he gradually advanced himself to be one of the firm. Of course,
his fortune then rose with the house, and his
wealth, at the time I saw him, was computed
at upwards of a hundred thousand pounds. Yet
I am sure that an old-clothes-man would not
have given half-a-crown for the whole of the
apparel (or rather rags) upon his back.

Now, as it is too often the custom with people, in forming an opinion, seldom to go beyond the surface, this modern AVARO was, by
many, termed *a man without pride!* Few
gave a guess at the real motive of all this
studied negligence. But those who investi-
gate the human character, and trace actions to
the secret springs of the heart, saw, in this
inattention to personal decency, the very
acmé of personal pride. I shall prove my position by repeating the usual reply of this old
man, when any of his acquaintance ventured
to enquire why he wore such tattered garments. " Why," he would answer, " were I

to dress as smart as other people, no one would know T. W. from another man."

Men may fall into this mistaken road to distinction, but women, who have suddenly become wealthy, seldom do. A passion for dress is so common with the sex, that it ought not to be very surprising, when opulence, vanity, and bad taste meet, that we should find extravagance and tawdry profusion the fruits of the union. And it would be well if a humour for expensive dress were always confined to the fortunate daughters of Plutus; but we too often find this ruinous spirit in women of slender means; and then, what ought to be one of the embellishments of life, is turned into a splendid mischief. Alas! my friends, it must have come under your own observations, that often does the foolish virgin or infatuated matron, sell her peace or her honour for a ring or a scarf!

A woman of principle and prudence must be consistent in the style and quality of her attire; she must be careful that her expenditure does not exceed the limits of her allowance. She must be aware, that it is not the

girl who lavishes the most money on her
apparel, that is the best arrayed. Frequent
instances have I known, where young women
with a little good taste, ingenuity, and economy, have maintained a much better appearance than ladies of three times their fortune.
No treasury is large enough to supply indiscriminate profusion; and scarcely any purse
is too scanty for the uses of life; when
managed by a careful hand. Few are the
situations in which a woman can be placed,
whether she be married or single, where some
attention to thrift is not expected. High rank
requires adequate means to support its consequence; ostentatious wealth, a superabundance to maintain its domineering pretensions;
and the middle class, when virtue is its companion, looks to economy, to allow it to throw
its mite into the lap of charity.

Hence, we see, that hardly any woman,
however related, can have a right to independent, uncontroled expenditure; and that,
to do her duty in every sense of the word, she
must learn to understand and exercise the
graces of economy. This quality will be a

gem in her husband's eyes; for, though most of the money-getting sex like to see their wives well-dressed, yet, trust me, my fair friends, they would rather owe that pleasure to your taste than to their pockets!

Costliness being, then, no essential principle in real elegance, I shall proceed to give you a few hints on what are the distinguishing circumstances of a well-ordered toilet.

As the beauty of form and complexion is different in different women, and is still more varied according to the ages of the fair subjects of investigation; so the styles in dress, while simplicity is the soul of all, must assume a character corresponding with the wearer.

The seasons of life should be arrayed like those of the year. In the spring of youth, when all is lovely and gay, then, as the soft green, sparkling in freshness, bedecks the earth; so, light and transparent robes, of tender colours, should adorn the limbs of the young beauty. If she be of the Hebe form, warm weather should find her veiled in fine muslin, lawn, gauzes, and other lucid materials. To suit the character of her figure, and to accord with the prevailing mode and just taste together, her morning robes should be of a length sufficiently circumscribed as not to impede her walking; but on no account must they be too short; for when any design is betrayed of showing the foot or ancle, the idea of beauty is lost in that of the wearer's odious indelicacy. On the reverse, when no show of vanity is apparent in the dress; when the lightly flowing drapery, by unsought accident discovers the pretty buskined foot or taper ancle, a sense of virgin timidity, and of exquisite loveliness, together strike upon the senses; and admiration, with a tender sigh, softly whispers, "The most resistless charm is modesty!"

The morning robe should cover the arms and the bosom, nay, even the neck. And if it be made tight to the shape, every symmetrical line is discovered with a grace so decent, that vestals, without a blush, might adopt the chaste apparel. This simple garb leaves to beauty all her empire: no furbelows, no heavy ornaments, load the figure, warp the outlines, and distract the attention. All is light, easy and elegant; and the lovely wearer, " with her glossy ringlets loosely bound," moves with the Zephyrs on the airy wing of youth and innocence.

Her summer evening dress may be of a still more gossamer texture; but it must still preserve the same simplicity, though its gracefully-diverging folds may fall like the mantle of Juno, in clustering drapery about her steps. There they should meet the snowy slipper, and the still more spotless foot. In this dress, her arms, and part of her neck and bosom may be unveiled: but only *part*. The eye of maternal decorum should draw the virgin zone to the limit where modesty would bid it rest.

Where beauty is, ornaments are unnecessary ; and where it is not, they are unavailing—but as gems and flowers are handsome in themselves, and when tastefully disposed, doubly so; a beautiful young woman, if she chuses to share her empire with the jeweller and the florist, may, not inelegantly, decorate her neck, arms, and head, with a string of pearls and a band of flowers.

Female youth, of airy forms and fair complexions, ought to reject, as too heavy for her style of figure, the use of gems. Their ornaments should hardly ever exceed the natural or imitated flowers of the most delicate tribes. The Snow-drop, Lilly of the Valley, Violet, Primrose, Myrtle, Provence Rose ; these, and their resemblances, are embellishments which harmonize with their gaiety and blooming years. The colours of their garments, when not white, should be the most tender shades of green, yellow, pink, blue, and lilac. These, when judiciously selected, or mingled, array the graceful wearer, like another Iris, breathing youth and loveliness.

Should a young woman, of majestic character, enquire for appropriate apparel, she will find it to correspond with her graver and more dignified mien. Her robes should always be long and flowing, and more ample in their folds than those of her gayer sister. Their substance should also be thicker, and of a soberer colour. White is becoming to all characters; and not less so to Juno than to Venus: but when colours are to be worn, I recommend to the lady of majestic deportment, to chuse the fuller shades of yellow, purple, crimson, scarlet, black, and grey. The materials of her dress in summer, cambrics, muslins, sarsenets; in winter, satins, velvets, broad cloth, &c. Her ornaments should be embroidery of gold, silver, and precious stones, with fillets and diadems of jewels, and waving plumes.

The materials for the winter dresses of majestic forms, and lightly-graceful ones, may be of nearly similar texture, only differing, when made up, in amplitude and abundance of drapery. Satin, Genoa velvet, Indian silks, and kerseymere, may all be fashioned into as becoming an apparel for the slender figure as for the more *en bon point;* and the warmth they afford is highly needful to preserve health during the cold and damps of winter.—When it is so universally acknowledged, the indispensable necessity of keeping the body in a just temperature, between heat and cold, I cannot but be astonished at the little attention that is paid to so momentous a subject, by the people of this climate. I wonder that a sense of personal comfort, aided by the well-founded conviction that health is the only preservative of beauty, and lengthener of youth, that it does not impel women to prefer utility before the absurd whims of an unreasonable fashion.

To wear gossamer dresses, with bare necks and naked arms, in a hard frost, has been the mode in this country ; and unless a principle is made against it, may be so again, to the utter wretchedness of them, who, so arraying their youth, lay themselves open to the untimely ravages of rheumatisms, palsies, consumptions, and death.

While fine taste, as well as fashion, decrees that the beautiful outline of a well-proportioned form shall be seen in the contour of a nicely-adapted dress, the divisions of that dress must be few and simple. But, though the hoop and quilted petticoat are no longer suffered to shroud in hideous obscurity one of the loveliest works in nature, yet all intermediate covering is not to be banished. Modesty, on one hand, and Health on the other, still maintain the law of " fold on fold."

Some of our fair dames appear, summer and winter, with no other shelter from sun or frost, than one single garment of muslin or silk over their chemise—*if they wear one!* but that is often dubious. The indelicacy of this mode need not be pointed out; and yet, O shame! it is most generally followed. However, common as the crime is, (for who will say that it is not a sin against modesty?) it is quickly visited with its punishment. It loses its aim, if it hopes to attract the admiration of manly worth. No eye but that of a libertine can look upon so wanton a figure with any other sensations than those of disgust and contempt: and the end of all her arts being lost, the certainty of an early old age, chronic pains and deeply-furrowed wrinkles, is thus incurred in vain.

No woman, even in the warmest flush of youth, ought to be prodigal of her charms; she should not " unmask her beauties to the

moon ;" or unduely expose the vital fluid,
which animates her frame with life and joy.
A momentary blast from the east may pierce
her filmy robes, wither her bloom, and lay
her low for ever.

The *Chemise*, (now too frequently banished,) ought to be held as sacred by the
modest fair, as the vestal veil. No fashion
should be able to strip her of that decent
covering; in short, women should consider it
as the sign of her delicacy, as the pledge of
honour to shelter her from the gaze of un-
hallowed eyes. There are circumstances
which might occur to her, wherein the want
of this decent garment might subject her to
a shame never to be forgotten by herself or
others. Let her think of accidents " by
flood, or field, or fire;" and I trust she will
never again subject herself to the chance of
such unwomanly exposure.

This indispensable vesture being once more
appropriated to its ancient use, we shall next
speak of the stays, or *corsets*. They must be
light and flexible, yielding to the shape,
while they support it. In warm weather, my

fair reader should wear under her gown and slip, a light cotton petticoat; these few habiliments are sufficient to impart the softening line of modesty to the defined outline of the form. Health, also, is preserved by their opposing the immediate influence of the atmosphere; and none will deny, that enough of female charms are thus displayed, to gratify the quick, discerning eye of taste.

During the chilling airs of spring and autumn, the cotton petticoat should give place to fine flannel; and in the rigid season of winter, another addition must be made, by rendering the outer garments warmer in their original texture: for instance, substituting satins, velvets, and rich stuffs, for the lighter materials of summer. And besides these, the use of fur is not only a salutary, but a magnificent and graceful appendage to dress.

Having laid it down, as a general principle, that the fashion of the raiment must correspond with that of the figure; and that every sort of woman will not look equally well in the same style of apparel, it will not be difficult to make you understand that a handsome per-

son may make a freer use of fancy in her
ornaments, than an ordinary one. Beauty
gives effect to all things; it is the universal
embellisher, the settling which makes common
crystal shine as diamonds. In short, fashion
does not adorn beauty; but beauty fashion.
Hence I must warn Delia, that if she be not
cast in so perfect a mould as Celia, she must
not flatter herself that she can supply the
deficiency by gayer or more sumptuous attire.
Whims in dress may possibly pass with her,
who, " in Parisian mode, or Indian guise, is
still the fairest fair!" But caprices of this
sort, in a plain woman, only renders her defects more conspicuous; and she who might
have been regarded as a very pleasing girl, in
an obtrusive robe of simple elegance, is ridi-
culed and despised, when descried in the inap-
propriate plumage of fancy and decoration.

Many men, while listening to the conversation of an ordinary, but sensible, young woman, would never see that her hair was harsh
and of a bad colour, were it not interwoven
with a wreath of roses. They would not perceive the brownness and want of symmetry

in her bosom, did not the sparkling necklace attract his eye to the spot. Neither would it strike him that her hands were coarse and red, did not the pearl bracelets and circles of rings tell him that she meant they should vie with Celia's rose-tipped fingers.

As I recommend a restrained and quiet mode of dress to plain women, so, in gradation as the lovely of my sex advance towards the vale of years, I counsel them to assume a graver habit and a less vivacious air. Cheerfulness is becoming to all times of life, but sportiveness belongs to youth alone; and when the meridian or the decline of our days affects it, is ever heavy and out of place.

Let me show you, my fair friends, by conducting you into the Pantheon of ancient Rome, the images of yourselves at the different stages of your lives. First, behold that lovely Hebe; her robes are like the air, her motion is on the zephyr's wing: that you may be till you are twenty. Then comes the beautiful Diana. The chaste dignity of the pure intelligence within pervades the whole form, and the very drapery which enfolds it, harmonizes with the modest elegance, the buoyant health, which gives elasticity and grace to every limb : here then you see yourselves from twenty to thirty. At that majestic age, when the woman of mind looks round upon the world; back on the events which have past, and calmly forward to those which may be to come; all within ought to be settled on the firm basis of religion and sound judgment; and either as a Juno or a Minerva she stands forth in the power of beauty and of wisdom. At this period she lays aside the flowers of youth, and arrays herself in the majesty of sobriety, or in the grandeur of simple magnificence.

Contradictory as the two last terms may at first appear, they are consistent; and a glance on the works of Phidias, and of his best imitators, will sufficiently prove their beautiful union. Long is the reign of this commanding epoch of a woman's age; for from thirty to fifty she may most respectably maintain her station on this throne of matron excellence. But at that period, when she has numbered half a century, then it becomes her to throw aside " the wimple and the crisping iron, the ornament of silver and the ornament of gold;" and gracefully acknowledging her entrance into the vale of years, to wrap herself in her mantle of grey, and move gently down till she passes through its extremest bourn to the mansions of immortality.

Ah! who is there amongst us, who, having once viewed the reality of this picture, would exchange such blessed relinquishment of the world and all its vanities for the bolstered back, enamelled cheek, and be-wigged head of a modern old woman just trembling on the verge of the grave, and yet a candidate for the flattery of men?

It has been most wisely said (and it would be well if the waning queens of beauty would adopt the reflection), that there is a *time for every thing!* We may add, that there is a time to be young, a time to be old; a time to be loved, a time to be revered; a time to seek life, and a time to be ready to lay it down.

She who best knows how to fashion herself

to these inevitable changes is the only truly, only lastingly fair. Her beauty is in the mind, and shown in action; and when men cease to admire the woman, they do better, they revere the saint.

ON THE PECULIARITIES OF DRESS, WITH REFER-ENCE TO THE STATION OF THE WEARER.

As there is a propriety in adapting your dress to the different seasons of your life, and the peculiar character of your figure, there is likewise a necessity that it should correspond with the station you hold in society.

This is a subject not less of a moral concern than it is a matter of taste. By the universality of finery and expensive articles in dress, ranks are not only rendered undistinguishable, but the fortunes of moderate families and of industrious tradesmen are brought to ruin: the sons become sharpers, and the virtue of the wives and daughters too often follows in the same destruction.

It is not from a proud wish to confine elegance to persons of quality that I contend for less extravagant habits in the middle and lower orders of people: it is a conviction of the evil which their vanity produces that impels me to condemn *in toto* the present levelling and expensive mode.

A tradesman's wife is now as sumptuously arrayed as a countess; and a waiting-maid as gaily as her lady. I speak not of our merchants, who, like those of Florence under the Medici family, have the fortunes of princes, and may therefore decorate the fair partners of their lives with the rich produce of the divers countries they visit; but I animadvert on our retail shopkeepers, our linen-drapers, upholsterers, &c. who, not content with gold and silver baubles, trick out their dames in jewels! No wonder that these men load their consciences with dishonest profits, or make their last appearance in the newspaper as insolvent or *felo de se!*

Should the woman of moderate fortune be so ignorant of the principles of real elegance as to sigh for the splendid apparels of the court, let her receive as an undeniable truth, that mediocrity of circumstances being able to afford clean and simple raiment, furnishes all that is essential for taste to improve into perfect elegance. Riches and splendour will attract notice, and may often excite admiration;

but it is the privilege of propriety and sweet retiring grace alone to rivet the eye, and take captive the heart.

> " Many there are who seem to shun all care,
> And with a pleasing negligence ensnare."

The fashion of educating all ranks of young women alike, is the cause why all ranks of women attempt to dress alike. If the brazier's daughter is taught to sing, dance, and play like the heiress to an earldom, we must not be surprised that she will also emulate the decorations of her rival. We see her imitate the coronet on lady Mary's brows; and though miss Molly may possibly not be able to have hers of gems, foil-stones produce a similar effect; then she looks for rings, bracelets, armlets, to give appropriate grace to the elegant arts she has learnt to practise; and when she is thus arrayed, she plays away the wanton and the fool, till some libertine of fortune buys her either for a wife or a mistress.

Were girls of the plebeian classes brought

up in the praise-worthy habits of domestic
duties; had they learned how to manage a
house, how to economize and produce comfort
at the least expence at their father's frugal yet
hospitable table ; we should not hear of dancing-masters and music-masters, of French and
Italian masters; they would have no time for
them.   We should not see gaudy robes and
glittering trinkets dangling on the counter, or
shining at a Sunday ordinary ; they would not
know where to shew them :—we should not be
told of seductions, or ruins ; the appearance
of these young women would not attract the
flatterer; and their simple hearts know not the
desires of luxury and vanity.

After having drawn this agreeable picture
of her who has well-chosen, I will leave this
modern daughter of industry to her discreet
and virtuous simplicity ; and once more turn
to her whose fortune and station render
greater change and expence in apparel not
only admissible but commendable.   A woman
with adequate means, when she fills an exten-

sive wardrobe, encourages the arts and manu-
factures of her country, and replenishes the
scanty purse of many a laborious family.

At this period of universal talent, articles of
dress may be purchased at a price so insignificant as hardly to be named, or at the vast
cost of half a fortune. A pretty muslin gown
may be bought by the village girl for ten shil-
lings; while a robe of the same material, but
of a finer quality, cannot be purchased by a
lady of rank for less than as many guineas.
Indian muslin wrought with gold or silver is
nearly as costly as the stately brocades of our
ancestors, but it is infinitely more elegant.

Indeed, when we look back upon their
heavy fashions we cannot but see that in almost every respect the advantage of the
change is on our side. With the stiffness of
cloth of gold and embroidered tissues, have
also disappeared the enormous pile of hair,
furbelows, feathers, diamond towers, windmills,
&c. which a certain witty poet used to denominate " the building of the head." Now,
easy tresses, the shining braid, the flowing

ringlet confined by the *antique* comb, or bod-
kin, give graceful specimens of the simple
taste of modern beauty. Nothing can correspond more elegantly with the untrammelled
drapery of our newly-adopted classic raiment
than this undecorated coiffure of nature.

While we find that the pious bishop Latimer
remonstrated with the females of his time
against the monstrous superfluity of their
" roundabouts, artificial hips, &c. &c." and
recommended to their use the " honest *single*
garment ;"—our moralists, equally pious, take
up the argument on the contrary side, and
justly condemn the too adhesive and transparent robe worn by our cotemporary belles !
On this subject we must dissent from the venerable reformer of the sixteenth century ; and
agree with those of the nineteenth, that the
single garment (as the texture now usually is)
is not a meet covering for a christian damsel.

I am sorry to be obliged to call to your observation, my gentle friends, that the modern
fair have deviated widely from that medium
between the Bacchante and the Vestal, which

a discreet candidate for admiration would wish to preserve. The nature of man is prone to extremes; and, flying from the heavy farthing-gale and the stuffed petticoat, women assume almost the Spartan guise; and, not meeting minds in the opposite sex as pure as those in Lacedæmon, no wonder that the chaste matron called upon to foretel the consequence should remain silent and veil her head.

" Good sense," says La Rochefoucault, " should be the test of all rule, whether ancient or modern. Whatever is incompatible with good sense must be false." Modesty should, on the same principle, be the test of the propriety of all personal apparel or ornament: for whatever is incompatible with her ordinances must degrade and betray.

Hence you will perceive, my young readers, that in no case a true friend or lover would wish you to discover to the eye more of the " form divine" than can be indistinctly descried through the mysterious involvements of, at least, three successive folds of drapery.

Love, friendship, and real taste, are alike delicate.

To the exposure of the bosom and back, as some ladies display those parts of their person, what shall we say ? This mode (like every other which is carried to excess and indiscriminately followed) is not only repugnant to decency, but most exceedingly disadvantageous to the charms of nine women out of ten. The bosom and shoulders of a very young and fair girl may be displayed without exciting much displeasure or disgust ; the beholder regards the too prodigal exhibition, not as the act of the youthful innocent, but as the effect of accident, or perhaps the designed exposure of some ignorant dresser. But when a woman, grown to the age of discretion, of her own choice " unveils her beauties to the sun and moon ;" then, from even an Helen's charms the sated eye turns away loathing. It has discerned the licentious heart beneath the swelling breast, and its beauties no longer captivate. Again, I repeat, the libertine, the gross Epicurean, may feast his imbruted gaze upon a form so stripped of decency ; for he is a creature whose senses are bent to the earth, and the basest offerings are his banquet. But a man of delicacy, of worth, turns from the couch of sensuality, though Venus herself reposed there ; and with celestial rapture clasps to his warm and noble heart the unsunned bosom of the chaste and vestal-enwrapped fair.

Were we even, in a frantic and impious passion, to set virtue aside, policy should direct our damsels to be more sparing of their attractions. An unrestrained indulgence of the eye robs imagination of her power, and prevents her consequent influence on the heart. And if this be the case where real beauty is exposed, how much more subversive of its aim must be the studied display of an ordinary or deformed figure ! The monstrous exhibition which some women make of their backs below the *scapula*, is a fashion that sets taste at defiance. Even with the fairest forms and finest skins this practice is injurious to the desired effect. It discovers a part of the shape which, if not seen wholly, (that is altogether with the whole of the well-shaped bust) is far from being pleasing. The beauty of the back depends upon the general outline seen at once, where, with a single glance, you can take in the finely undulating line which, gently swelling from muscle to muscle, completes the perfect form. However, bad as the taste is in this respect, we must congratulate ourselves that vanity has not yet trod so far on modesty as to make her votaries unveil themselves to the waist.

Judgment, as well as decency, declares, that it is sufficient in evening and full-dress to disrobe the back of the neck to the top of the delicate undulation on the rise of the shoulder. Women, according to the fineness of their skins and proportions, must accept or decline the privileges which modesty grants. It is preposterous for her who is of a brown, dingy, or speckled complexion, to disarray her neck and arms as her fairer rival may. A clear brunette has as much liberty in this respect as the fairest; but not so the muddy-skinned and ill-formed. A candid consideration of our pretensions on these subjects, and an impartial judgment, must decide our style of apparel; and consequently our respectability with the discerning.

Perhaps it is necessary to remind my readers that custom regulates the veiling or unveiling the figure, according to different periods in the day. In the morning the arms and bosom must be completely covered to the throat and wrists. From the dinner-hour to the termination of the day, the arms, to a graceful height above the elbow, may be bare; and the neck and shoulders unveiled as far as delicacy will allow.

The bosom, which nature has formed with exquisite symmetry in itself, and admirable adaption to the parts of the figure to which it is united, has been transformed into a shape, and transplanted to a place, which deprives it of its original beauty and harmony with the rest of the person. This hideous metamorphose has been effected by means of newly invented stays or corsets which, by an extra-ordinary construction and force of material, force the figure of the wearer into whatever form the artist pleases.

A vile taste in the contriver, and as stupid an approval by a large majority of women, have brought this monstrous distortion into a kind of fashion ; and in consequence we see, in eight women out of ten, the hips squeezed into a circumference little more than the waist; and the bosom shoved up to the chin, making a sort of fleshy shelf, disgusting to the be-holders, and certainly most incommodious to the bearer.

Curiosity may incline you to wish to know something of these buckram machines, that you may form an idea of their intention, use, or rather inutility. I will satisfy you by de-scribing them to the best of my power.

The leader in this arming phalanx is usually called the *long stay*. And its announcement to the female world, if not by drum or trum-pet, furnishes not only much matter for ora-tory in the advertisement, but a no inconsider-

able fund of merriment to the readers of these
curious performances. For instance, " Mrs.
and Miss L. P. have willed it, and it is done at
their house, &c. &c." here follows a list of
their *improved long stay, pregnant stay, divorces,*
&c. &c. O! female delicacy, where is thy
blush when thou lookest on such exposure of
the chaste reserves of thy person!

The first time my eye met these words so
coupled, I was seized with that honest shud-
dering which every delicate woman ought to
feel at seeing the parts and situations of her
person, which modesty bids her conceal, thus
dragged before the imagination of the opposite sex. The pure must read it with the frown
of disgust, the impure with the smile of ridicule.
To this moment (though I find that nothing
disrespectful to modesty was *meant* by the advertisement) I cannot approve the terms in
which it is written ; for, it is my opinion (and
I am so happy as to be supported in it by the
sanction of the wisest moralists), that, rob
woman of her delicate reserves, and you take
from her one of the best strongholds of her

chastity. You deprive her of her sweet attractive mysteries; you lay open to the eye of love
the arcana of her toilet, the infirmities of her
nature; the enchantment is broken, and "the
bloom of young desire, the purple light of the
soul's enthusiasm," expire at the disclosure.

To please my still-curious readers I will
still farther displease myself, and enter more
circumstantially into a detail of these strange
appendages to the female wardrobe.

But before I proceed with my remarks on
the *long stay* (the ringleader of the rest), I will
so far rescue the intention of its constructors
from any *design* to excite improper ideas by
the words of their advertisement, as to ex-
plain to you the proposed usefulness of the in-
ventions denominated *pregnant stay* and *divorces.*

The first is a *corset* or *stay* of dimity, or
jean, or silk; reaching from the shoulders,
down the waist, and over the hips, to the complete envelopement of the body. It is rendered of more than ordinary power by elastic
bones, &c. which, introduced between the

lining and covering of the *stay*, bring it to something like the consistence and shape of an ancient warrior's hauberk. This new-fashioned coat-of-mail for the fair sex is so constructed as to compress and reduce to the shape desired the natural prominence of the female figure in a state of fruitfulness. Some women, who are bold enough to wear this Procrustean garb during every stage of their pregnancy, affirm that it preserves the shape without injury to their state of increase. However this may be with a few hardy individuals, I profess myself no proselyte to the innovation ; as it must necessarily put a degree of restraint upon the operations of nature, very likely to produce bad effects both on the mother and the child.

Support and confinement to an overstrained part are two different things ; the one is beneficial, the other destructive. And this I can assure my readers, that I ever have remarked that those married women who have longest maintained their virgin forms were those who, in a state of maternal increase, observed a proper medium between a too relaxed and a too contracted boddice.

Nature in these concerns is our best guide; and, when she dictates to us to provide against the possible disagreeable consequences of any of her operations, it is well to obey her; but when a fastidious, and, allow me to say, an indelicate regard to personal charms would excite you to brace with ribs of whalebone the plastic mold of your unborn infant; or when it has, in spite of these arts, burst its prison-house alive, you seek to deprive it of the nourishment your breast prepares; then remember, that you perform not the duty of a mother, but show yourself rather egregiously guilty of wantonness and unpardonable cruelty.

The next ill-named thing I have to describe is the article of apparel called the *divorce*. This title is even more shocking than the foregoing; and I confess I should not think the woman who could have the face to enquire for it far from giving a specimen of a different meaning to the same word in a different place.

This supposed auxiliary to female loveliness is, like its type in Doctors' Commons, designed, most unnaturally, to separate what the hand of their Creator had brought into most graceful union. It consists of a piece of steel or iron, of a triangular form, gently curved on each side. This formidable breast-plate (for the attraction of love's arrows, not to repel them!) is covered with soft materials; and thus bedded, placed in the centre of the chest to divide the breasts. I have heard of the cestus of Venus as the talisman of beauty; of the girdle of Florizel, the pledge of female honour; and the zone of Serena, the band of gentleness and love ! But of this iron investment I never heard till now; and from certain deductions, I can pronounce that it possesses not one of the virtues so eminent in its three classic predecessors.

I pause upon my pen while I muse on what my youthful readers will think when they have

read the foregoing description. Can they believe that I am writing of an article of dress belonging to modest women? they must suppose
I am depicting the meretricious arts of some
courtezan : it cannot be the delicate virgins,
the discreet matrons of a land famed for female decorum, that I am thus holding up to
public censure! Even so. When the soul is
forgotten in the catalogue of our charms, no
wonder that the body should be made all in
all. When a wife prefers the tumults of passion, before the tenderness of love, can we be
surprised that she assumes the garb of Thais,
the artifice of a —— my pen refuses to write
the epithet; but you will not be at a loss to
complete the sentence.

No person living can feel a more lively admiration than that which animates me at the
sight of a beautiful form. I behold in it the
work of a most perfect being; the accomplishment of one of His fairest designs : He seems
to shew in earthy mold the lovely transcript of
the angels of heaven; she looks, she breathes
of innocence and sweet unconscious beauty.

But when I cast my eyes on women issuing from the house of a modern manufacturer of shapes; when I see the functions of nature impeded by bands and ligatures; when I behold the abode of virgin modesty, the tender mother's fountain of aliment for her new-born babe, thrust forward to the gaze of the libertine; when I observe the pains taken to attract his eye—I turn away disgusted; I blush for my sex, and cannot forbear to cry aloud, " Oh, that my daughters were hidden from the face of man, and of woman too, that they might never witness such prostitution of the female form!"

Vile as these meretricious arts are, they are not less dangerous to health than to morals. The constant pressure of such hard substances as whalebone, steel, &c. upon so susceptible a part as the bosom is very likely, in the course of a very short time, to produce all the horrid consequences of abscesses, cancers,&c.; on their miseries I need not to descant.

On the *long stay* (in distinction from the *pregnant stay*) I shall now make a few re-

marks, arising from the observations I have been
enabled to make on the ladies of various ages
and figures whom I have known wear it. To the
woman whose waning charms set in an ex-
uberance of flesh, perhaps the support of this
adventitious aid is an advantage. But in that
case its stiffening should rather be cord quilted in the lining, or very thin whalebone, than
either steel or iron. In all situations the boddice should be flexible to the motion of the
body and the undulations in the shape; and it
should never be *felt* to *press* upon any part.

Thus far we may tolerate the adoption of
this buckram suit for elderly or excessively
en bon point ladies; but for the *growing* girl
(who, I am sorry to say, mothers not unfrequently imprison in these machines) it is
both unrequired and mischievous.

Before nature has completed her work in
the perfection of the youthful figure, she is
checked in her progress by the impediment
which the valves, bands, &c. of the *long stay*
throw in her way. Those finely rounded
points which mark the distinction and the

grace of the female form, and which the artist, enamoured of beauty, delights to delineate with the nicest accuracy—are, by the constant pressure of these *stays*, rendered indistinct, and in a short time are entirely destroyed.

Let then the *long stay* be restricted to the too abundant mass of fattening matronhood: so may art restrain the excesses, not of nature, but of disease. Unwieldy flesh was never yet seen in a perfectly healthy person: it generally arises either from intemperance overloading the functions of life, or dissipation decomposing them.

Let the *padded corset* rectify the defects of the deformed. But where nature has given the outline of a well-constructed form, forbear to traverse her designs. Youth should be left to spring up unconfined like the young cedar; and when the hand of man, or accident, does not distort the pliant stem, it will grow erect and firm, spreading its beautiful and cheerful shade over the heads of its planters.

ON THE DETAIL OF DRESS.

THERE are few things in which our sex can discover more taste than in the choice of the apparel which may best accord with their several styles of figures and features; but we frequently see the direct opposite of good judgment in their selections, and behold between the person and the attire a complete and laughable incongruity.

Some women will actually disguise and disfigure themselves rather than not appear in the prevailing fashion; which, though advantageous to one character of face, may have the direct contrary effect with another. I hinted at this in the earlier part of this dissertation. Now I come closer to my subject; intending to enter into a minute detail of what ought or ought not to be worn by women of different molds and complexions.

If Daphne have the features of a Siddons, and Amaryllis those of a Jordan, the style which agrees with the one must ill accord with the other. The like harmony must be maintained between the complexion and the colours we wear. For it is these minutiæ which, like the nice and almost imperceptible touches of the ingenious artist, produce a complete and faultless whole. That a handsome woman may disfigure herself by an injudicious choice or disposition of her attire; and a plain one counteract the errors of nature, so as to render herself at least agreeable; almost every experienced observer has witnessed. We may therefore conclude, that beauty with a bad taste is far less desirable than a good taste without beauty.

" What an awkward creature is that !" said a gentleman to me the other evening at a supper, and pointing to a *slatternly* beauty who sat opposite, with her chin nearly reposing on her bosom, and her shoulders drawn up almost to her ears. " Yonder is a very elegant woman !" observed he, directing my attention to a lady who, critically considered, was rather ordinary; but by her judicious style of dress, her unstudied graces of deportment, claimed universal admiration.

To support my arguments with those of a lady whose taste is best evinced by her own personal elegance, I shall give you a short extract from a little tract of hers, which, like the divine Psyché of Mrs. Taite, has been only permitted to meet the eyes of a favoured few.

" Who is there among us that has not witnessed a beautiful woman so apparelled as to render her rather an object of pity and ridicule than of admiration ? How often do we see simplicity and youthful loveliness obscured by a redundancy of ornaments ! How often do the robust and healthy, the majestic and the gay, the pensive and the sportive, follow the same mode ; marring, mingling, and mangling without mercy, and without taste ; regardless of discrimination, appropriation, or judgment ; to the total overthrow of the attractions which nature liberally bestowed ! Do not these ladies perceive that each style of personal beau-

ty has a distinct character to support? That
a tasteful adaption will enforce the stamp
which nature has impressed? Let us then admonish the female whose beauty is of the fair,
pale, and interesting cast, not to render her
appearance insipid by the overpowering hues
of robes, mantles, pelisses, &c. of amber,
orange, grass-green, crimson, or rose-colour.
This soft style of beauty makes its appeal to
our most delicate perceptions : all grossness of
colour displeases them; and therefore should
not be admitted in the articles of her dress.

" Grass-green, though a colour exceedingly pleasing and refreshing in itself, jaundices
the complexion of the pale woman to such a
degree as to excite little other sensations
in the beholder than compassion for the poor
invalid. Such females should in general choose
their robes of an *intire colour;* and when they
wear white garments they should animate
them with draperies, mantles, scarfs, ribbons,
&c. of pale-pink, blossom-colour, celestial
blue, lilac, dove-colour, and primrose; leaving
full green, deep blue, and purple to the florid;

and amber, scarlet, orange, flame-colour, and
deep rose, to the brunette.

" Thus much we offer in the suitable ap-
propriations of colours. We shall now proceed to say something on the prevailing fashions of the day; and though we may fairly
congratulate our countrywomen on their taste
and improvement in this particular, yet here
also the regulating hand of judgment, the nice
and discriminating effects of genius, and the
directing influence of a delicate and just taste,
become most importantly necessary.

" The mantle, or cottage-cloak, should never be worn by females exceeding a moderate
en bon point ; and we should recommend their
winter garbs, such as Russian pelisses and
Turkish wraps, to be formed of double sarsnet, or fine Merina cloth, rather than velvets,
which (except black) give an appearance of
increased size to the wearer. In the adoption
of furs, flat-ermine or fringe fur is better suited to the full-formed woman than swan's-
down, fox, chinchilli, or sable; these are graceful for the more slender. Women of a spare

habit, and of a tall and elegant height, will derive considerable advantage from the full-flowing robe, mantle, and Roman tunic. The fur trimming, too, gives to them an appearance of roundness which nature has denied ; and to this description of person we can scarcely recommend an evening-dress more chaste, elegant and advantageous, than robes of white satin trimmed with swan's-down, with draperies of silver or gossamer net. The antique head-dress, or queen Mary *coif*, is best adapted to the Roman and Grecian line of feature. The Chinese hat and Highland helmet are becoming to countenances of a rounder and more playful contour.

" We have frequently, in our observations, found occasion to lament in the present style of female dress a want of that proper distinction which should ever be attended to in the several degrees of *costume.* For instance, the short gown, so appropriate and convenient for walking and pursuing morning avocations or exercises, intrudes beyond its sphere when seen in the evening or full dress, It is

in the splendid drawing-room that the train
robe appears with all that superiority which
gives preeminence to grace, and dignity to
beauty.

" Why should these pleasingly-varying distinctions be neglected? The long sleeve, too,
(now so universal in almost every order of
dress) belongs with strict propriety only to
the domestic habit. These are inattentions or
faults which a correct taste will quickly discover and easily rectify. It is dangerous to
level distinctions in one case, and disadvan-
tages in the other. There should be a just
and reasonable discipline in trifles, as well as
in matters of higher import. There is a vast
deal more in things of seeming insignificance
than is commonly imagined. Subjects of importance, high achievements, and glorious
examples, strike every beholder; but there are
few who reflect that it is by perseverance and
attention to comparative trifles that mighty
deeds are performed, and that great consequences are ultimately produced.

" A correct taste is ever the concomitant of

a chaste mind ; for, as a celebrated author has justly observed, *our taste commonly declines with our merit.* A correct taste is the offspring of all that is delicate in sentiment and just in conception : it softens the inflexibility of truth, and decks reason in the most persuasive garments.

" A walking-dress cannot be constructed too simply. All attractive and fancy articles should be confined to the carriage-dress, or dinner and evening apparel. We shall here particularly address the order of females who may not have the luxury of a carriage, and yet be within the rank of gentlewomen. This class composes treble the number of those to whom fortune has bestowed the appendages of equipages and retinue. We shall in our observations particularly aim at increasing their respectability, by leading them to adopt a style of adornment which, while it combines fashion and elegance, shall be remarkable only for its neatness and simplicity.

" It has been said that the love of dress is

natural to the sex: and we see no reason
why any female should be offended with the
assertion. *Dress*, says an author on the subject, *is the natural finish of beauty. Without
dress a handsome person is a gem, but a gem
that is not set.* Dress, however, must be subject to certain rules; be consistent with the
graces, and with nature. By attention to
these particulars is produced that agreeable
exterior which pleases, we know not why;
which charms, even without that first and
powerful attraction, beauty.

"Fashion, in her various flights, frequently
soars beyond the reach of propriety. Good
sense, taste, and delicacy, then make their appeal in vain. Her despotic and arbitrary
sway levels and confounds. Where is delicacy? where is policy? we mentally exclaim,
when we see the fair inconsiderate votary of
fashion exposing, unseemly, that bosom which
good men delight to imagine the abode of innocence and truth. Can the gaze of the voluptuous, the unlicensed admiration of the

profligate, compensate to the woman of sentiment and purity for what she loses in the estimation of the moral and the just?

" But, delicacy apart, what shall we say to
the blind conceit of the robust, the coarse,
the waning fair-one, who thus obtrude the ravages of time upon the public eye? Let us
not offend! We wish to lead to conviction,
not to awaken resentment. Fashion must, in
these instances, have borrowed the bondage of
fortune, and so blinded her votaries against
the sober dictates of reason, the mild dignity
of self-respect.

" There is a mediocrity which bounds all
things, and even fixes the standard which di-
vides virtue from bombast. Let us, therefore,
in every concern endeavour to observe this
happy temperature. Let the youthful female
exhibit without shade as much of her bust as
shall come within the limits of fashion, without infringing on the borders of immodesty.
Let the fair of riper years appear less exposed.
To sensible and tasteful women a hint is
merely required. They need not very close

instruction; for at once they perceive, com-
bine, and adopt, with judgment and delicacy.
The rules of propriety are followed, as it were,
instinctively by them ; and their example is so
impressed on the generality of our lovely countrywomen (who, too often and inconsiderately,
follow the vagaries of fashion with, perhaps,
ridiculing avidity) that we thus take upon us
to correct the irregularities of the many, in
hopes that the judicious few will embrace
grace and make it universal.

" Far be it from us to lead the female mind
from its solemn engagements to the pursuit of
comparative nothings. But there is a time
and a place for all things, and for every innocent purpose, under heaven; and on these
grounds we do not see why a female should
not blend the agreeable with the estimable.

" There are persons who neglect their dress
from pride, and a desire to attract by a careless singularity : but wherever this is the case,
depend on it something is wrong in the mind.
Lavater has observed that persons habitually
attentive to their attire display the same re-

gularity in their domestic affairs. *Young wo-men*, he continues, *who neglect their toilet, and manifest little concern about dress, indicate a general disregard of order ; a mind but ill-adapted to the detail of house-keeping ; a deficiency of taste, and of the qualities that inspire love :—they will be careless in every thing. The girl of eighteen who desires not to please will be a slut or a shrew at twenty-five. Pay attention, young men, to this sign ; it never yet was known to deceive.*

" Hence we see that the desire of exhibiting an amiable exterior is essentially requisite in woman. It is to be received as an unequivocal symbol of those qualities which we seek in a wife : it indicates cleanliness, sweetness, a love of order and of universal propriety. What, then, is there to censure in a moderate consideration of dress !—Nothing. We may blame when we find extravagance, profusion, misappropriation ; the tyranny of fashion, slavery to vanity ; in short, bad taste !

" Let us then urge the British fair to that elegant simplicity, that discriminating selection, which combines fashion, utility, and grace. Thus shall the inventive faculty of genius be honoured and encouraged; and industry receive the reward of its ingenuity and labours.

" We shall now proceed to notice the present articles which claim fashionable preeminence, and give some useful hints on their application.

" As a walking habit we know of none in summer which is more graceful than the lightly flowing shade of lace or finest muslin. And in winter no invention can exceed the Trans-Baltic-coat or Lapland-wrap. These comfortable shields from the cold are usually formed of cloth or velvet, with deep collars and cuffs of sable, or other well-contrasted fur. Ladies of the first nobility usually have them lined throughout with the same costly skins. These garments wrap over the figure in front; sometimes they have them without other ornament than their bordering furs; and at others, fasten them with magnificent clasps and buckles. We have seen one of these coats (or, as northern travellers denominate them, *shoubs*) on a female of high rank, composed of crimson velvet, with deep cuffs, cape, and collar of spotted ermine, and a deep border of the same down the sides. It had a superb effect; and with the imperial helmet-hat of the same material, exhibited one of the most sumptuous carriage *costumes* that can be imagined.

" When this dress is adopted by the pedestrian fair, we recommend it to be of a more sober hue, and that the bonnet should be of the provincial poke or cottage form.

" Short women destroy the symmetry of their forms, and encumber their charms, with redundancy of ornament, either in their morning or evening attires. A little woman befeathered and furbelowed looks like a queen of the *Bantam* tribe; and we dare not approach her for fear of ruffling her plumes. Feathers are much in vogue; and though formerly a symbol of full dress, are now often a mark of graceful negligence, and are seen falling carelessly, and floating with ease: they kiss the rosy cheek of youth and health; or, less courteous, steal the vermilion from the painted face of fading maturity, as fanned by the spiteful breeze they wave from her bonneted head in the gay promenade.

" We love to see our countrywomen remarkable for elegance and modesty, as well as beauty. Englishmen, accustomed to objects of undisputed loveliness, aim at something beyond the surface of external charms ; they require that all should be fair within.

" Hear what a male writer has observed on the fashion of exposing the bosom ! *A woman, proud of her beauty,* says he, *may possibly be nothing but a coquet: one who makes a public display of her* bosom, *is something worse.* This writer insinuates too much ; for we believe that so far from our females being actuated in this case by any unbecoming motive, they too commonly act from no motive at all ; save that blind and mistaken one which we have so much condemned—*the heedless adoption of an absurdity, because it is the fashion !* But let the inconsiderate beauty remember, that where two motives can be assigned to an action, the world will generally adopt that which is least favourable!"

Though I have made this extract, which enters so intimately into the secrets of the toilet, and descants so engagingly on its attractive subject, I must desire that it may not be supposed I would seek to create an inordinate degree of care respecting that which is comparatively of no account, when placed in competition with the indispensable qualities and acquirements which ought to adorn the christian maid. I would have my fair friends be fully impressed with the truth, that it is not she who spends the most time at her toilet that is usually the best dressed : a too zealous care generally subverts the effect it was meant to produce. A multiplicity of ornaments ever distract the attention, and detract from feminine loveliness. They are regarded as a sort of *make weights* in a scale, where nature must have been a niggard to render them necessary.

In the like manner a diversity of colours
bespeaks vulgarity of taste, and a mind without innate elegance or acquired culture.
Where doubt may be about this or that hue
being becoming or genteel (as it is very possible it may neither be the one nor the other),
let the puzzled beauty leave both, and se-
curely array herself in simple white. That
primeval hue never offends, and frequently
is the most graceful robe that youth and
loveliness can wear. " It is inconceiva-
ble," says a writer on the subject, " how
much the colour of a gown or a shawl may
heighten or destroy the beauty of a complexion; and how much the sex in general
neglect these (to them) important particulars." Every consideration must yield to the
prevailing mode ; and to this tyrant all advantages are sacrificed. Women no longer consult their figures, but the whim of the moment ; and it is sufficient for them that the
Duchess of D——, or the Marchioness of
E——, appeared in *murry*-colour or *coqueli-*

cot, to make all the *belles* in England, black, brown, or fair, array themselves in the same livery.

Nothing contributes more to the setting forth of the beauties of a complexion than the choice of the colours opposed to it. Women should not only be nice in this adaption, but they must be careful that the different shades or hues they admit in the various parts of their garments should accord with each other.

Here it is that we distinguish the woman of taste from the hoyden ready to empty a pedlar's pack upon her shoulders. To attempt to contrast two shades of the same colour has in general a very harsh effect; indeed I never saw it harmonize in the least, except in the case of two greens as a trimming; or in the beautiful blending of nature in the form and hues of flowers.

It is also not unworthy of remark, that colours which are to make a part of evening apparel ought to be chosen by candle-light; for if in the morning, forgetful of the influence of

different lights on these things, you purchase
a robe of pale yellow, purple, lilac, or rose colour, you will be greatly disappointed when at
night it is observed to you that your dress is
either dingy, foxy, or black.

The harmonious assortment of well-chosen
colours was once quite a science amongst
women: and even now it may not only be
considered as a specimen of delicate taste, but
a proof of that genius which, if cultivated,
might distil the hues of Iris over the animated
canvass fraught with beauty and life.

This union of a thousand dyes " by nature's pure and cunning hand laid on," cannot be found in greater perfection than in the
resplendent lap of summer; then the earth
teems with gay enchantment, and presents to
the fair wanderers through her fragrant bowers
the loveliest raiment for their beauties. This
animating and native ornament, so interesting
and charming in itself, should ever find a place
on the toilet of youth. How can a beauteous
young woman (the fairest production of creation) be more suitably adorned than with this

sweet apparel of the fairest season? Flowers
recal so many pleasing images to the mind,
that when a beholder sees them he is ever put
in a temper to admire; and, when they are
found blended with the beauties of a lovely
girl, the effect is irresistible.

The simple wreath of roses, the jessamine,
the lily of the valley, the snow-drop, the brilliant ranunculus, and a long train of rival
sweets, offer themselves at the shrine of female
taste. From this rich assemblage are selected and formed those delicious garlands which
deck the snowy brows of Celia, which twine
with Chloe's golden hair. From this fair par-
terre we collect the variegated *bouquet*, which,
reposing on the bosom of beauty, mingles its
fragrant breath with hers.

This tender, this exquisite sweetness, which
we inhale from the lily, the rose, or the violet,
is far preferable to all the extracted perfumes
that ever were wafted " from Indus to the
pole." They are not only purer and more
balmy; but, when on approaching a lovely

woman, we find, not only our eye delighted with the sight of beauty, but our senses "wrapped in the sweet embrace of soft perfumes;" when it is not the preconcerted fragrancy of essences drawn from east to west, and poured upon the fair with the design to *affect our senses;* then we yield ourselves to the lovely breathing of nature. We see her in the charming creature before us, blooming in youth and freshness; we feel her in the thousand odours of Paradise emanating from the newly-plucked flowers, which, being nature's offspring, as well as herself, seem to share her being, imbibing and partaking sweetness.

Amidst the variety of materials with which women decorate their persons, there is not one that requires greater discrimination in the use than those articles of jewelry which we denominate trinkets. Here good taste, the general regulatrix, now resumes her sway. The blind directress of the luxuriant imagination gives grace to solidity, and consequence to trifles. Her magic spirit breathes in the laurels of the hero, dwells on the lip of oratory, and sparkles in the gem that decorates the fair!

To women of the most exalted as well as of the more humble ranks we recommend a moderate, rather than a profuse, display of conspicuous and shewy ornaments. A well-educated taste ought to open the eyes of a woman to be a tolerably correct judge of the perfections or imperfections of her own person; and by that judgment she ought to regulate the adoption or rejection of striking decoration.

It is well to remind my youthful reader that she can never learn these truths (when they are on the defective side) but from the decisions of her own impartial mind. Few women, much less men, would venture to say to an improperly dressed young lady,—"Madam, your fingers are too clumsy to wear with advantage that brilliant ring;—your neck and arms are too meager, discoloured, or coarse, to adopt the pearl bracelet or necklace; unless indeed you soften the contrast by putting a lace shirt and long sleeve between your skin and the pearls." These observations would place the too frank adviser in a similar situation with that of *Gil Blas* when correcting the manuscripts of the conceited *prelate of Granada ;*—and, therefore, we cannot expect that any friend would run the risk of incurring our resentment, when they might retain our favour by only permitting us to make ourselves as ridiculous as we please.

Let me then, in the light of an *author* who cannot be supposed, in a general address, to mean any individual personal reflections, admonish my readers, one and all, not to neglect composing their complexions with the hues and brilliancy of the gems offered to them to wear. Clear brunettes shine with the greatest lustre when they adopt pearls, diamonds, topazes, and bright amber. The fair beauty may also wear all these with advantage, while she exclusively claims as her own emeralds, garnets, amythists, rubies, onyxes, &c. &c. Cornelian, coral, and jet, may be worn by either; but certainly produce the most pleasing effect on the rose and lily complexion.

Ornaments and trimmings of silver are to be preferred before gold when intended for the fair beauty. The white lustre of the first of these costly metals harmonizes better with delicacy of skin than the glaring effulgence of the gold. By a parity of reasoning, gold agrees best with the brunette, as its yellow and flaming hue lights up the fire of her eyes, and throws her complexion in the brightest contrast.

If the *clavicle*, or collar-bone, be too apparent, either from accidental thinness or original shape, remedy the defect by letting the necklace fall immediately into the cavity which the ungraceful projection occasions. But should this bone protrude itself to an absolutely ugly extent, I would recommend the neck to be completely covered by a lace handkerchief and frill; for its exposure would only give a bad specimen of a figure which may be

in every other part of a just and fine proportion.

If the prevailing fashion be to reject the
long sleeve, and to partially display the arm,
let the glove advance considerably above the
elbow, and there be fastened with a drawing-
string or armlet. But this should only be the
case when the arm is muscular, coarse,
or scraggy. When it is fair, smooth, and round,
it will admit of the glove being pushed down
to a little above the wrists.

There is perhaps no single beauty of the
female form which obtains so much admiration
as a well-proportioned foot and ancle. Possibly the liveliness of this sentiment may be
increased in this instance by the rarity of
the perfection being found amongst the British
fair.

There is a *je ne scai quoi* in a fine ancle,
which seems to assure the gazer that the
whole of the form of which it is a sample is
shaped with the same exquisite grace. A
heavy leg and foot seems to hint that the
whole of the limbs which the drapery conceals

are in gravitating proportion with their clumsy foundations: and where we see ponderosity of body, we are apt to conclude that there is equal heaviness in mind and feelings. This may be an unjust mode of reasoning, but it is a very common one; and so I account for the general prejudice against any unusual weight in the lower extremities.

When we consider that it required the famous sculptor of Greece to collect the most beautiful virgins from every part of his country before he could find a living model for every part of his projected statue of perfect beauty; when we consider this, that the very native land of female charms could not produce one woman completely faultless in her form; how can we be so unreasonable as to demand such perfection in a daughter of Britain?

Let not the other sex scrutinize too closely, nor demand that universal and correct symmetry in their wives and daughters which was never yet found but in the elaborately chiseled models of the sculptor's study.

It must not, however, be presumed from what I have said that the generality of other countries are happier in the beautiful formation of their women's forms than England; or that the British fair are at all more notorious than many other nations for heavy feet and legs. So far from it, there are ladies in England with feet and ancles of so delicate a symmetry, that there is nothing in modelling or in marble to excel their perfection. But to make a display of them; to exhibit them by unusually short petticoats; and draw attention by extraordinary gay attire; is an instance of immodesty and ill-taste which attracts to the vain coquet contempt instead of admiration. Men despise her for her impropriety; and envious women have a fair subject on which to ground their detractions.

In short, it can never be sufficiently inculcated that modesty is the most graceful ornament of beauty.

Be the foot eminently handsome, or the reverse, it alike requires to be arrayed soberly. Except on certain brilliant occasions, its shoe should be confined to grave and clean-looking colours; of the first, black, greys and browns; of the last, white, nankeen, pale blue, green, &c. according to the colour of the dress and the time of day. I should suppose it almost useless to say, that (except in a carriage) the dark colours ought to be preferred in a morning. To be sure there is nothing out of character in wearing nankeen shoes or half-boots in the early part of the day, even in walking, provided the other parts of your dress be spotless white, or of the same buff hue. The other delicate colours I have mentioned above (I repeat, except in a carriage) are confined to evening dresses. Red Morocco, scarlet, and those very vivid hues cannot be worn with any propriety until winter, when the colour of the mantle or pelisse may sanction its fulness. On brilliant assembly nights, or court drawing-rooms, the spangled or diamond-decorated slipper has a magnificent and appropriate effect. But for the raiment of the leg, we totally disapprove, at all times, of the much ornamented stocking.

The open-wove clock and instep, instead
of displaying fine proportion, confuse the
contour; and may produce an impression of
gaiety; but exclude that of beauty, whose rays
always strike singly. But if the clock be a
coloured or a gold one, as I have sometimes
seen, how glaring is the exhibition! how
coarse the association of ideas it produces in
the fancy! Instead of a woman of refined
manners and polished habits, your imagination
reverts to the gross and repelling females of
Portsmouth-point, or Plymouth-dock; or at
least to the hired opera-dancer, whose business it is to make her foot and ancle the principal object which characterizes her charms,
and attracts the *coup d'œil* of the whole assembly.

If I may give my fair friends a hint on this
delicate subject, it would be that the finest
rounded ancles are most effectually shown by
wearing a silk stocking *without any clock.* The
eye then slides easily over the unbroken line,
and takes in all its beauties. But when the
ancle is rather large, or square, then a pretty

unobtrusive net clock, of the same colour as
the stocking, will be a useful division, and induce the beholder to believe the perfect symmetry of the parts. A very thick leg cannot
be disguised or amended; and in this case I
can only recommend absolute neatness in the
dressing of the limb, and petticoats so long
that there is hardly a chance of its ever being
séen.

One cause of *thick ancles* in young women
is want of exercise, and abiding much in over-
heated rooms. Standing too long has often
the same effect, by subjecting the limb to an
unnatural load, and therefore to swelling. The
only preventive or cure for this malady is a
strict attention to health You might as well
expect to see a rose-bush spring, bud, and
bloom, in a closely-pent oven, as anticipate
fine proportions and complexion from a long
continuance of the exotic fashions of these
days.

If a girl wishes to be well-shaped and well-
complexioned she must use due exercise *on
foot.* Horseback is an excellent auxiliary, as

it gives much the same degree of motion, with double the animation, in consequence of the change of air and variation of objects: but carriage exercise is so little, that we cannot recommend it to any case that is short of an absolute invalid. A woman in respectable health must *walk* to maintain her happy temperament. By this she will still more consolidate her solids, and preserve the shape with which nature has kindly endowed her. If it was originally fine, fine it will remain; and if it was but ordinary, it will at least save itself from growing deformed.

Indolence (which is want of action) deranges the functions of nature. Disease is engendered: sometimes it shews itself in acute and constant disorders of the alimentary organs, which produce leanness and a skeleton-form; but most often it decomposes the solids (which would otherwise have swoln to graceful projection, and brought to the admirable point of insertion the braced muscle); and reducing flesh to fat, and consistency to fluid, presents to your eye, instead of the airy nymph, and gracefully *en bon point* matron, the unwieldy, the swoln, the dropsical valetudinarian!

Health is the mother of beauty, decency her governess, taste and judgment her attendants. Remember this, my fair readers; and, as Cicero said of *action*, so say ye of the essentials of your charms. What is the eloquence of your beauty?—Modesty! What is its first argument?—Modesty! What is its second?—Modesty! What is its third?—Modesty!—What is its peroration, the winding up of all its charms, the striking spell that binds the heart of man to her for ever?—Modesty!!!

Modesty is all in all; for it comprises the beauties of the mind as well as those of the body; and happy is he who finds her!

ON DEPORTMENT,

HAVING discoursed so largely on form and
apparel, I shall now throw together a few
hints on that indispensable assistant-grace of
beauty, an elegant and appropriate air.

This subject should be particularly considered; and the arguments from such reflections strongly enforced on the attention of
young women. There is scarcely an observer
of manners and their effects who will not
maintain that the most beautiful and well-
dressed woman will soon cease to please unless
her charms are accompanied with the ineffable
enchantment of a graceful demeanour. A
pretty face may be seen every day, but grace
and elegance, being generally the offspring of
a polished mind, are more rare; and are consequently more distinguished.

While we exult in the preeminent beauty
of our fair countrywomen; while we talk of
their lilies and roses, and downy skins; we

cannot but shrink from comparison when we bring their manners in parallel with the females of other nations who have not half their corporeal advantages.

I am not going to deny that in this land of beauty (a land to which a certain cardinal, many centuries ago, gave the appellation of *the native paradise of angels!*) we shall find the fair " fitted or to shine in courts, or walk the shade with innocence and contemplation joined." There are many lovely women of all ranks in England who merit this encomium: but I am not writing a eulogium on these happy exceptions, I feel it my duty to admonish the general race of my female cotemporaries. To the rising generation I especially address myself; and when the young belle in her teens listens to the suggestions of experience, perhaps the advice may not be quite so unpalatable when she understands that it comes from one who has studied the graces at more than one of the courts of the Bourbons; and, since their dispersion, has followed the flight of elegance wherever it was to be found.

As lessons are best taught by example, I will, for a few minutes, turn back upon my steps of former years; and for the sake of edifying my young friends give them a slight sketch of the appearance and manners of the most distinguished women I met in the various realms I have visited.

As Paris was the first foreign court to which I was presented, I will give it that precedence which it certainly deserved under the magic sway of the beautiful, and since unfortunate, Antoinette. In speaking of perfection of manners I shall not select as examples queens and princesses; the sphere in which they move demands an entirely different air from that of ladies who, however exalted in rank, are yet daily in the habit of meeting equals and superiors. On these grounds I shall not discourse on the mien of the queen of France, or the deportment of madame Elizabeth; my model for Parisian elegance was the young and charming Comtesse de M. She was of a moderate stature, her shape easy, and her complexion of a clear brown, brightened by a rouge not so strong as

to give any degree of *fierté* to her intelligent
and animated eyes. Her figure being light and
sylphic, her step and air possessed a bounding
and sportive elasticity, which kept her ever in
a motion that enchanted the senses with the
same delight we feel in viewing the careless
evolutions of an unaffected and accomplished
dancer in a graceful ballet. Her manners in
all respects harmonized with this ever-varying mien. She played on several instruments
with knowledge sufficient never to displease.
Her vivacity, temperated by her carelessness;
her performing by starts, as the whim seized her;
her snatching the vocal lute, flying to the
piano-forte, or instantly warbling a lively
song, gave to the whole a charm that was
truly irresistible. Never seeming to seek
admiration, she was always sure to find it;
appearing to receive pleasure from every object that approached her sphere, she imparted
a corresponding animation to all around: and
while passing negligently on, with the unobserv-
ing enjoyment of a child, every eye sought her,
every foot followed her, as the very source of

pleasure, the fountain where sprang their rare and innocent delight: such was this lovely comtesse. Like other young married women united by parents to a man she knew not, she was surrounded by lovers; but no infectious sighs ever invaded the pure atmosphere of her charms; all around her was smiles and hilarity. The men who admired her soon found that gallantry formed no part in her angelic constitution; and wearing the name which custom gave them with thoughts as spotless as her own, they contemplated her graces, united in her sports, and became happy with innocence.

My next visit was paid to Spain and Portugal. The most agreeable woman I met at Madrid was the only daughter of the Conde di P. Donna Victoria was tall and slender, with a complexion so dark, that none could look on her without being reminded of her Moorish ancestors. But with this Ethiopian hue, she, like Cleopatra, brought conquerors to her feet; and, like Aspasia, melted the frozen heart of age and austerity with her mental charms. Victoria was not better

instructed in literature than are the generality
of her countrywomen. She was a *devotée*, but not
with the ascetic ideas of a cloistered religionist:
her devotion warmed her heart, and animated
her genius; it seemed to raise her soul to
heavenly courts, or to draw down the inhabitants of Paradise to abide on earth with her.
She would at times talk with the animation of
angels, and the canonized host of sainted
virgins, which would have almost persuaded
you that she had indeed been already admitted
to their seraphic choirs. This feature in her
character gave a particularly celestial air to
her etherial form; and as I have seen her sitting, on a fine glowing evening, beneath the
shade of a far-spreading orange-tree, and bending over the Manzanares, with her mandolin
in her hand, chaunting her vesper-hymn to the
virgin, I have almost fancied her the tutelary
angel of Spain invoking the Deity to make all
its daughters resemble her spotless self. She
was also far read in Spanish romance; and
the high heroic strain which such pictures gave
to her ever-meditative mind, operating on a

soul naturally framed for greatness, completed a character in the eighteenth century which is supposed never to have existed since the days of the crusades. This extraordinary creature's air and deportment were in perfect harmony with the high tone of her thoughts: it was the step of a superior being, and every movement declared the mental beauty and graceful tranquillity within. Her voice was irresistibly commanding and persuasive; and her eyes, which were large, full, and beaming with intelligence, seemed to pour out a soul full of benevolence and great resolve upon all around. Princes bowed before her as they would before an angel; but she saw none who came up to the image a (perhaps) too-refined taste had drawn in her heart, and at a very early age she died in a convent.

At the court of the Braganzas I met with a far different belle, the young widowed Duchesse di A. She was of so petite a figure as rather to look like a fairy than a woman; but then it was queen Mab full of sports and wiles; it was Titonia, the very dictatress of the hearts of

men. She possessed no more education
than what lay in her guitar and her dancing-
master ; but in these two arts she was admirable. Her madrigal was unequalled, and many
a despairing lover passed from under her midnight window enraptured with the magic touch
of her finger, the joy-inspiring cadence of her
voice. Her peculiar grace and agility in the
active and expressive movements of the fandango and bullero would force to admiration
the most insensible beholder; and the gaiety
and apparent undesigningness of her manners,
while they betrayed our confidence, took captive our souls. Women loved her as the most
ingenious of women; men adored her as the
most disinterested of mistresses. Her lively
olive complexion was rendered brilliant by the
animating colour of health, and of a dazzling
splendor by the vivacity of her speaking black
eyes: all conspired to form a face of such gay
associations, and withal so amiable, that envy
never reached her, and reproach died away in
her presence. Her deportment was gay and
simple; it was that of a joyous child of nature,

with her heart ever in her hand; you might read its contents, and with no unwelcome pencil write your own lineaments there.   Had virtue been the companion of these *agremens* she would have been a perfect model of female simplicity and charms; but, alas! the passion for gallantry, so common with her country-women, was inherent in her: and, like the butterfly, she sipped the flowers of the neighbouring gardens without the proprietors being conscious of their loss.   Her intrigues, like her nature, were volatile; and rumour had hardly caught the tale before she had passed to another object; hence few believed the scandal, and least of all the abused wife or mistress of the faithless lover.   I knew this woman and loved her, till an accident convinced me of her systematic frailty; and from that hour until now I have driven her seductive witcheries from my memory.

At the court of Naples I found the manners still more amatory than at that of Lisbon. Turn where I would I could discover none but the slightly-veiled votaries of the Paphian goddess; some appeared more like the declared priestesses of her shrine than her mysterious visitants: and I should have left Naples in disgust, had not our ambassador, by (what I deemed a happy) accident, presented me one evening, in a party of pleasure over to Sicily, to the celebrated Marchesa di V. The splendor of her charms rivetted my attention. I had seen statues of the queen of beauty, I had read of the variety of her enchantments; but surely until now I could never have expected to see such divine loveliness realized on earth! All that poets have ever dreamt of female perfection was to be found in her face and figure: such exquisite proportion, such graceful symmetry of limbs; such an assemblage of the most lovely features, with a complexion which seemed to have been painted by the gods themselves! all combined to make me gaze on her with admiration. But when she moved, when she spoke, when she sang, when she conversed, it was grace, it was eloquence, it was music, it was an overflow of sentiments and feeling to set the soul in a

blaze: not mine, for I am of a temperate
construction, but the men who were with
me, two of whom were English and one
French; they were captivated, entranced. I
remained a week in this syren's company, and
at the end of it I departed with my French
companion alone. He had been satiated with
the marchesa's charms, and wise enough
to leave her; but one of my two British friends
lay wounded by the other's hand; and on so
sad a bed of repentance lamented the art of
the female libertine, who, for the pleasure of a
single moment of gratified vanity, exulted in
seeing the friendship of years divided by the
duelist's steel.

It was with gratitude to my kind destiny
that I left this profligate scene to witness the
soberer *agremens* of Vienna. The Baroness
Saxe W. here became my friend. I com-
menced my acquaintance with her on the death
of her only daughter, an infant of two years
old. The baroness was not then more than
twenty. In all my journeyings to and fro
upon the earth I never saw such female dignity,

such gentle majesty of manners: while she looked up to her husband as to her legitimate lord, and obeyed the wish of his eye with the alacrity of duty and fondness; the chastened command of her aspect to all under her authority; the dignified suavity of her deportment to her acquaintance, which invited confidence and enjoined respect; all united, made me see in her the true model of wives, mistresses, and friends.

Cautiously I began my acquaintance with her, although the sensibilities of nature awakened my sympathy with the sorrowing mother of a dead child. I partook her grief; but I would not share my heart with her till I was convinced that in her bosom virtue was united with feeling. A year's intimacy convinced me of this; and after five-and-twenty years of the closest interchange of thoughts, I now find that of all my female friends she is the most charming, most consistent, and most exemplary.

I afterwards passed through Switzerland and Holland, and found the women in each simple, honest, and amiable. I never reached Russia, Sweden, or Denmark; but I am told that the ladies in these countries very much resemble those of England. Like them they are fair, reserved, and chaste; and, like them, often cold, awkward, and repelling.

"Cold, awkward, and repelling!" Can a modern frequenter of certain gay votaries in London read this sentence, and see any likeness between it and any of the fair-ones he meets there? Instead of the maidenly coldness which used to distinguish the women of England, we see girls too wanton for restraint; we behold women so inflamed with the worst passions, that no laws, human or divine, can hold them within bounds!

The *awkward, reserved* air of the early part of the last century has given way, not to *grace* and *frankness*, but to an *unblushing impudence*, which is the very assassin of female virtue and connubial honour. Think not I am too severe, ye indulgent mothers! regard me not as a cynic, ye thoughtless daughters of imitation! I mean not to arraign your hearts, but your manners; I seek to pluck the garb of Phryné from your chaste and christian shoulders. Who, that is an actress, when called upon to perform the part of spotless *Virginia*, would rush upon the stage half naked, dancing, rolling her eyes as if intoxicated, and flirting with every officer of the *pretorian guard* who crossed her path? In such a case, should we not call the actress mad; or say, " If such were Virginia, he performed a rash and unnecessary act who avenged the insulted person of such a wanton on the first magistrate of Rome!"

Yet such Virginias are our Virginias! and to see a modest, abashed, retiring, blushing girl enter one of our assemblies is as uncommon a sight as now and then an embassy from a foreign land. The modern taste for exhibition of all kinds is the chief source of this depravity; a girl is no longer taught to dance that she may move easily in the occasional festivities of her neighbourhood, and enjoy the graceful exercise of a birth-day or a race ball, without annoying the movements of her companions. No! these are not sufficient: she takes her lessons of the *corps de ballet*, that she may present herself in the ball-room or on a stage; and while the motions of her limbs and the exposure of her person scandalize every discreet matron present, she believes herself the object of general admiration, the very *ne plus ultra* of the art. In like manner her musical talents are cultivated. She does not learn to compose with her sweet lullaby the unquiet hours of old age, or of sickness, to rest and sleep: enough for her relations, father, brothers, husband, that she practises all day the crude and disagreeable parts of her lessons. It is for the guest, the gay assembly, the concert of *amateurs* that she reserves her harmonies, and to them she sings and plays till she believes *herself* the tenth muse, and *them* her adorers.

Can we be surprised that from such an education should be produced the vain, the conceited, the presumptuous, the impudent!

To check this growing evil by showing the young candidate for admiration what is "woman's best knowledge and her praises;" to show her what is indeed the proper, the graceful, the winning deportment, is the design of these few following pages; and I trust that my young reader will receive them as the admonition of a tender and experienced parent, and not allow " a mother's precepts to be vain!"

Having laid it down as a first principle, that no demeanour, whether in a princess or a country-girl, can be becoming that is not grounded in *feminine delicacy,* I shall proceed to show that a different deportment is expected from different persons. Certain characteristics of persons are suited to certain styles of manners; and also the same demeanour does not agree as well with the steward's daughter as the squire's bride.

As in a former chapter I have particularized the dresses which are adapted to the gay and the grave, so in the next I propose pointing out the appropriate miens which belong to the various degrees of beauty and classes of society.

PECULIARITIES IN CARRIAGE AND DEMEANOUR.

As order is the beautiful harmonizer of the universe, so consistency is the graceful combiner of all that is in woman to perfection.

In reference to this sentiment, her manners must bear due affinity with her figure, and her deportment with her rank. The youthful and delicate shaped girl is allowed a gaiety of air which would ill-become a woman of maturer years and larger proportions; but at all times of life, when the figure is slender, with a swan-like neck, and the motions are naturally swaying, for that girl or that woman to affect what is called a majestic air, would be as unavailing as absurd. It is not in the power of a figure so constructed ever to look majestic. By stiffening her joints, walking with an erect mien, and drawing up her neck, she would certainly be upright; she would seem to have had a determined dancing-master, who, in spite of nature and grace, had made her *hold up her head;* but she would never look like any thing but a stiff, inelegant creature. The character of these slight forms corresponds with their resemblances in the vegetable world: the aspen, the willow, bend their gentle heads at every passing breeze, and their flexible and tender arms toss in the wind with grace and beauty: such is the woman of delicate proportions. She must enter a room either with the buoyant step of a young nymph, if youth is her passport to sportiveness; or, if she is advanced nearer the meridian of life, she then may glide in, with that ease of manner which gives play to all the graceful motions of her elegantly undulating form. For her to crane up her neck would be to change its fine swan-like bend into the scraggy throat of the ostrich: all her movements should be of the same flexible character. Her mode of salutation should be rather a bow than a courtesy; and when she sits, she should model her easy attitude rather by the ideas of the painter, when he would portray a reclining nymph, than according to the lessons of the grace-destroy-governess, who would marshal her pupils on their chairs like a rank of drilled recruits. In short, for a slender or thin woman to be stiff at any time, is, in the first case, to render of no effect the advantages of nature; and in the next, to increase her defect, by making it more conspicuous by a constrained and over-ridiculous carriage.

Though we cannot unite the majestic air which declares command with this easy, nymph-like deportment, the dignity of modesty may be its inseparable companion. The timid, the retreating step, the down-cast eye, the varying complexion, " blushing at the deep regard she draws!" all these belong to this class of females; and they are charms so truly feminine, so exquisitely lovely, that I cannot but place them with their counterpart, the ethereal form, as the perfection of female beauty.

The woman whose figure bears nature's own stamp of majesty, is generally of a stately make; her person is squarer, and has more of *embonpoint* than the foregoing. The very muscles of her neck are so formed as to show their adaption to an erect posture. There is a sort of loftiness in the natural movement of her head, in the high swell of her expansive bosom. The step of this woman should be grave and firm; her motions few and commanding, and the carriage of her head and person erect and steady. An excess in stateliness could not have any worse effect on her, than perverting the majesty of nature into the haughtiness of art. We might admire or revere the first; the last we would probably resent and detest. The dignified beauty must therefore beware of overstraining the natural bent of her character: it is like the bombast of exalted language, which never fails to lose its aim and engender disgust. We might laugh at a delicate girl, so far exaggerating the pliancy of her form and ease of manners as to twist herself into the thousand antics of a Columbine; she aims at pleasing us, and though she chuses the wrong method, we will not frown, but only smile at the ridiculous exhibition. But when a majestic fair one presumes to arrogate an undue consequence in her air, it is not to gratify our senses that she assumes

the extraordinary diadem ; and, irritated at
the contempt her greatness would wish to
throw upon us, inferior personages, we treat
her like an usurper ; and, armed with a sense
of injustice, we determine to pull her at once
from her throne.

The easy, graceful air, we see, belongs exclusively to the slender beauty ; and the moderated majestic mien to a greater *embonpoint.*

There is a race of women whose persons
have no determined character. These must
regulate and adopt their demeanours according
to the degrees in which they approach the
two before-mentioned classes. But in all
cases, let it never be forgotten, that a too faint
copy of a model is better than an overchar-
ged one. Excess is always bad. Moderation
never offends. By falling easily into the degree of undulating grace, or the dignified de-
meanor which suits your character, you merely put on the robe which nature designed, and
the habit will fit and be becoming.

But when the nymph-like form assumes a
regal post, or a commanding dame pretends

to " skip and play," the affectation on both sides is equally absurd : discords of this kind are ever ridiculous and odious. Besides these, there are affectations of other descriptions, of equal folly and bad effect. Some ladies, to whom nature has given a good sight and lovely orbs to look through, must needs pretend a kind of half-blindless, and they go peeping about through an eye-glass, dangling at the end of a long gold chain, hanging at their necks. Not content with this affectation of one defect, they assume another, and lisp so inarticulately, that hardly three words in a sentence are intelligible. All such follies as these are not more a death-blow to all respect for the novice that plays them off, than they are sure antidotes to any charms she may possess. Simplicity is the perfection of form; simplicity is the perfection of fine dressing; simplicity is the perfection of air and manners.

In the details of carriage, we must not omit a due attention to gait and its accompanying air. We find that it was " by her *graceful walk* the Queen of Love was known !" In this

particular, the French women far exceed us.
Pope observes, that "they move easiest who
have learnt to *dance.*" And it is the step of
the highly-accomplished dancer that we see
in the generality of well-bred French women ;
not the march of the military serjeant, which
is the usual study with our pedestrian graces.
There is a buoyant lightness, a dignified ease
in the walk of a lady, who has been taught
the use of her limbs by a fine dancer, which
is never seen in her who has been drilled by
the halbert, and told to *stand at ease* with her
hands resting on her stomach, as if reposing
on the trigger of her firelock. Such a way
as we have fallen upon to teach our daughters
the *graceful step of the Queen of Love,* is, indeed, so singular, that until another race of
Amazons arise, to whom military tactics may
be useful, we have no chance of any imitators.
Indeed the marching walk of Englishwomen
is so ridiculous, even in the eyes of their own
countrymen, that I remember being one day
in St. James's Park, with one of these female
recruits, when a sentinel, with a humorous gravity, struck his musket to her as she passed.

Both in the case of air and gait, it is necessary to begin early to train the person and the limbs to the ease and grace you wish. It is difficult to straighten the stem long left to diverge into irregular wildness; but the tender tree, pliant in youth, needs only the directing hand of a careful gardener to train it to symmetry and luxuriance.

Many of the naturally most pleasing parts of the female shape have I seen assume an appearance absolutely disgusting; and all from an *outré* air, vulgar manners, or hoydening postures. The bosom, which should be prominent, by a lounging attitude sinks into slovenly flatness, rounding the back and projecting the shoulders! On the one side, I have seen a finely-proportioned figure transform herself into a perfect fright by this awkward neglect of all propriety and grace; and, on the other, I am acquainted with a lady whose beauty, taken in the common acceptation of the word, would not obtain her a second look, but in the elegance of her manners, in the dignity of her carriage, in the taste and disposition of her attire, and in the thousand

inexpressible charms which distinguish the
gentlewoman, she is so powerful that none can
behold her without captivation.

A late author, in a work entitled, " Remarks
on the English and French Ladies," very ably
points out the superior attention which the
women of France pay to the cultivation of
their air and manners; and he proceeds, with
no inconsiderable degree of eloquence, to exhort the British fair not to lose, by a careless
neglect, the advantages which nature has
given them over the *belles* of *la grande nation.*

" It must not be dissembled," says this writer, "that our much fairer countrywomen (the
English) are too often apt to forget that native charms may receive considerable improvement by attending to the regulation of carriage and motion. They ought to be reminded, that it is chiefly by an attention of this
kind, that the Frenchwomen, though unable
to rival them in such exterior perfections as
are the gift of nature, attain, however, to a
degree of eminence in other accomplishments,
that effaces the recollection of their inferiori-
ty of personal charms." He proceeds to ob-

serve that " the gracefulness of a French
lady's step is always a subject of high com-
mendation in the mouth of even Frenchmen;"
and, again, he says, " conscious where their
advantage lies, they spare no pains to improve
that grace of manner, that fund of vivacity,
which are in their nature so agreeable, and
which they know so well how to manage to
the best effect."

My intimacy with the French manners
makes me quote these short extracts with
greater pleasure ; and, as I bear witness to the
truth of their evidence, I hope that an amiable ambition will unite in the breasts of the
British fair, to be as much superior to their
French rivals, in all feminine graces, as our
British heroes are to the French on the seas !
We shall then see cultivated understandings,
unaffected cheerfulness, and manners of an
enchantment not be to exceeded by the fairest sorceresses in beauty and grace.

Sorceresses I would make you, my gentle
friends; but your spells should be those of
nature and of virtue. While I exhort you to
preserve your persons in comeliness, to array

yourselves in elegance and sweet attractive
grace, I would not lead you to believe, that
these are all of your charms, that these are
sufficient " to take the captive soul of love,
and lap it in Elysium !" No ; woman was
created for higher attainments ; many a heart
was formed to pant for dearer joys than these
can produce. Woman must, in every respect, and at all times, regard her form as a
secondary object; her mind is the point of
her first attention ; it is the strength of her
power; it is the part that links her with angels ; and, as such, she must respect, cultivate, and exalt it.

But as these familiar pages are expressly
intended as a little treatise on the dress of
these admirable qualities, I do not suppose it
demanded of me to enter so minutely into the
subject of mind, as I otherwise should have
esteemed it my duty. We have before admitted that, while on this earth, wandering
amongst the erring and voluptuous sons of
men, virtue must be clad in an attractive garb,
else few will love her for herself. To this
end then, like Solon of Athens, I give the

best directions the inmates of this gay world are capable of receiving; though, perhaps, not the best I could lay down. I would win the too earth-clinging soul by his senses, to give up his sensual enjoyments, and, caught by earthly charms, see and feel his connection, and, leaving the grosser part, aspire to mingle being with those alone which partake of immortality.

It is not by the showy attire of meretricious splendor, by the seductive air of Sybaritical refinement that I would effect this. " It is good that virtue keep ever with its like !" my means should ever be consistent with their object. So, with me, beauty, elegance, and grace, should be the only pleaders for the empire of morals and religion. On these principles, as I am aware that the most estimable and amiable qualities adorn the wives and daughters of our isle, I cannot but be the more solicitous that their outward deportment and appearance should exhibit a fair specimen of their inward worth.

" An upright heart and sensibility of soul are doubtlessly the most noble qualifications in the

fair sex. These, Englishwomen possess in
an eminent degree. But there are lighter
and perhaps more catching attractions, which,
though they will not bear a competition, are
nevertheless great smoothers of the rough
passages of life, and very necessary condu-
cives to social happiness.''

It is the opinion of wiser heads than mine,
that no circumstance, however trifling in itself, should be neglected, which strengthens
the bonds of an honourable and mutual attachment; and so great is the privilege allowed for this purpose, that it is deemed laudable
in woman to collect into herself all the innocent advantages, mentally and corporeally,
which may render her most admirable and
precious in the eyes of him who may be, or
is, her husband.

This latter sentiment reminds me to impress
upon my young friend, that there are shades
of demeanour which must be varied according
to the sex, degree, and affinity of the person
with whom she converses. To men of all
ranks and relations, she must ever hold a reserve on certain subjects, and indeed on al-

most every occasion, that she does not deem
necessary to observe with regard to her own
sex. To inferiors of both sexes she must
ever preserve a gracious condescension; but to
the men, a certain air of majesty must be
mixed with it, that she need not assume to the
women. To her equals, particularly of the
male sex, her manners must never lose sight
of a dignity sufficient to remind them that she
expects respect will be joined with probable
intimacy. In short, no intimacy should ever
be so familiar as to allow of any infringement
on the decent reserves which are the only pre-
servers of refinement in friendship and love.
What are called *cronies* amongst girls, are
among the worst of connections, as they generally are the very hot-beds of fancied love-
fits, secrecies, and really vulgar tale-bearing.

" Celestial Friendship!—
When e'er she stoops to visit earth, one shrine
The goddess finds, and one alone, to make
Her sweet amends for absent heaven,
The bosom of a friend, where heart meets heart,
Reciprocally soft—
Each other's pillow to repose divine!"

This friendship is indeed the gift of Heaven; a boon, more precious than much fine gold; but it is not usually to be found in school *cronies*; or, in the confidences of misses, whose unbosomings usually consist of flirtations, complaints against parents and guardians, and schemes for future parties of pleasure. Friendship is too sacred for these pretenders; under her influence " heart meets heart," and acknowledges her as the pledge of Heaven to man, of immortality, and endless joys. To such an intimate your whole soul may be laid open. But such an intimate is rare: you may meet her once in the shape of a female friend, and in that of a tender husband! But, believe not that her appearance will be more frequent. Hers are

" Like angel's visits, few and far between !"
Earth would be too much like heaven, were it otherwise.

To the generality then of your equals, while you are affable and amiable with them all, you must be intimate with few, and preserve an ingenuous reserve with most. Show them your sense of propriety demands a certain distance, and with redoubled respect they will yield what you require. With men of your acquaintance, you ought to be more reserved than with women. But while I counsel such dignity of manners, you must not suppose that I mean starchness, stiffness, prudery. I only recommend the modesty of the virgin; the sober dignity of matron years.

The present familiarity between the sexes is both shocking to delicacy and to the interest of women. Woman is now treated by the generality of men with a freedom that levels her with the commonest and most vulgar objects of their amusements. She is addressed as unceremoniously, treated as cavalierly, and left as abruptly as the veriest puppet they could pick up at Bartholomew Fair.

We no longer see the respectful bow, the look of polite attention, when a gentleman approaches a lady : he runs up to her, he seizes her by the hand, shakes it roughly, asks a few questions, and, to show that he has no interest in her answers, flies off again before she can make a reply.

To cure our coxcombs of this conceited impertinence, I would strongly exhort my young and lovely readers to treat them with the neglect they deserve. When any man, who is not privileged by the right of friendship or of kindred, to address her with an action of affection, attempts to take her hand, let her withdraw it immediately with an air so declarative of displeasure, that he shall not presume to repeat the offence. At no time ought she to volunteer shaking hands with a male acquaintance, who holds not any particular bond of esteem with regard to herself or family. A touch, a pressure of the hands, are the only external signs a woman can give of entertaining a particular regard for certain individuals. And to lavish this valuable power of expression upon all comers, upon the impudent and contemptible, is an indelicate extravagance which, I hope, needs only to be exposed, to be put for ever out of countenance.

As to the salute, the pressure of the lips : that is an interchange of affectionate greeting or tender farewell, sacred to the dearest connections alone. Our parent; our brothers; our near kindred; our husband; our lover, ready to become our husband; our bosom's inmate, the friend of *our heart's care;* to them are exclusively consecrated the lips of delicacy, and woe be to her who yields them to the stain of profanation!

By the last word, I do not mean the embrace of vice; but merely that indiscriminate facility which some young women have in permitting what they call a *good-natured kiss.*— These *good-natured kisses* have often very bad effects, and can never be permitted without injuring the fine gloss of that exquisite modesty which is the fairest garb of virgin beauty.

I remember the Count M——— ———, one of the most accomplished and handsomest young men in Vienna; when I was there, he was passionately in love with a girl of almost peerless beauty. She was the daughter of a man of great rank and influence at court, and on these considerations, as well in regard to her charms, she was followed by a multitude of suitors. She was lively and amiable, and treated them all with an affability which still kept them in her train, although it was generally known that she had avowed a predilection for Count M. and that preparations were making for their nuptials. The Count was of a refined mind and delicate sensibility: he loved her for herself alone; for the virtues which he believed dwelt in her beautiful form; and, like a lover of such perfections, he never approached her without timidity; and when he touched her, a fire shot through his veins, that warned him not to invade the vermilion sanctuary of her lips. Such were his feelings when, one night, at his intended father-in-law's, a party of young people were met to celebrate a certain festival; several of the young lady's rejected suitors were present. Forfeits were one of the pastimes, and all went on with the greatest merriment, till the Count was commanded, by some witty Mademoiselle, to redeem his glove, by saluting the cheek of his intended bride. The Count blushed, trembled, advanced to his mistress, retreated, advanced again—and at last, with a tremor that shook every fibre in his frame, with a modest grace,

he put the soft ringlet, which played upon her
cheek, to his lips, and retired to demand his
redeemed pledge in evident confusion. His
mistress gaily smiled, and the game went on.
One of her rejected suitors, but who was of a
merry, unthinking disposition, was adjudged,
by the same indiscreet crier of the forfeits,
[" as his last treat, before he hanged himself,"
she said]—to snatch a kiss from the lips of the
object of his recent vows. A lively contest
between the lady and the gentleman lasted for
a minute; but the lady yielded, though in the
midst of a convulsive laugh. And the Count
had the mortification, the agony, to see the
lips, which his passionate and delicate love
would not allow him to touch, kissed with
roughness and repetition by another man, and
one whom he despised. Without a word, he
rose from his chair, left the room—and the
house; and, by that *good-natured kiss*, the
fair boast of Vienna lost her husband and her
lover. The Count never saw her more.

ON THE MANAGEMENT OF THE PERSON IN DANCING,
AND IN THE EXERCISE OF OTHER FEMALE ACCOM.
PLISHMENTS.

IT is vain to expend large sums of money and
large portions of time in the acquirement of
accomplishments, unless some attention be
also paid to the attainment of a certain grace
in their exercise, which, though a circumstance distinct from themselves, is the secret
of their charm and pleasure-exciting quality.

As dancing is the accomplishment most calculated to display a fine form, elegant taste,
and graceful carriage to advantage; so towards it, our regards must be particularly
turned: and we shall find that when Beauty,
in all her power, is to be set forth, she cannot
chuse a more effective exhibition.

By the word *exhibition*, it must not be understood that I mean to insinuate any thing
like that scenic exhibition which we may expect from professors of the art, who often, regardless of modesty, not only display the

symmetry of their persons, but indelicately expose them, by most improper dresses and attitudes, on the public stage. What I propose by calling dancing an elegant mode of showing a fine form to advantage, has nothing more in it, than to teach the lovely young woman to move unembarrassed and with peculiar grace through the mazes of a dance, performed either in a private circle, or a public ball.

It must always be remembered, and it cannot be too often repeated, "That whatever it is worth while to do, it is worth while to do *well.*" Therefore, as all times and nations have deemed dancing a salubrious, decorous, and beautiful exercise, or rather happy pastime and celebration of festivity; I cannot but regard it with particular complacency. Dancing carries with it a banquet, alike for taste and feeling. The spectator of a well-ordered English ball sees, at one view, in a number of elegant young women, every species of female loveliness. He beholds the perfection of personal proportion. They are attired with all the gay habiliments of fashion and

of fancy; and their harmonious and agile
movements unfold to him, at every turn, the
ever-varying, ever-charming grace of motion.

Thus far his senses only are gratified.   But
the pleasure stops not there. His best feelings
receive their share also.   He looks on each
gay countenance, he sees hilarity in every
step; he listens to their delighted converse,
communicated by snatches; and, with a pleasure sympathizing with theirs, he cannot but
acknowledge that dancing is one of the most
innocent and rational, as well as the most
elegant, amusement of youth.

It is indeed the favourite pastime of nature.
We find it in courts, we meet it on the village
green.   Here the rustic swain whispers his
ardent suit to his blushing maid, while his
beating heart bounds against hers in the swift
wheel of the rapid dance.   There the polished
courtier breathes a soft sigh into the ear of
the lady of his vows, as he and she timidly
entwine their arms in the graceful *allemande*.

In every age of fashion, but the present,
dancing was as much expected from young
persons of both sexes, as that they should join

in smiles when mutually pleased. In days of yore, in the most polite eras of Greece and Rome, and of the chivalrous ages, we find that dancing was a favourite amusement with the first ranks of men. Kings, heroes, and un-bearded youth, alike mingled in the graceful exercise. Even in our own island, we read of the splendid balls given by our Plantage-nets and Tudors; and that every prince and nobleman contended in happy rivalry who should best acquit themselves in the dance. Here it was that the royal Harry lost his heart to the lovely Anna Bullen: and in such scenes did the gallant lords of his virgin daughter's court breathe out their souls at the feet of British beauty.

Such was the court of England! but now, where is " the merry dance, the mirth-awa-kening viol?" In vain our princes led forth their royal sisters and the fairest ladies in the land to celebrate, with festive steps, the birth-day; our noble youth, smit with a love of grave folly, abandon the ball for the gaming-table. The elegant society of the fair is dis-regarded and exchanged for fellowship with grooms and masters of the whip.   Shame on them! I cannot discant farther on such vulgar desertion of all that is lovely and decorous.

Besides the royal Brothers, a few yet remain amongst the young men of our higher ranks, who, in this respect, set a worthy example to the youth of inferior stations; and them we still meet at the assemblies of taste, moving with propriety and elegance in the social dance.   To make acceptable partners in the minuet, cotillion, &c. with these yet loyal votaries of Terpsichore, I beg leave to offer a few hints to my gentle readers!

Extraordinary as it may seem, at a period when dancing is so entirely neglected by men in general, women appear to be taking the most pains to acquire the art.   Our female youth are now not satisfied with what used to be considered *a good dancing-master;* that is, one who made teaching his sole profession; but now our girls must be taught by the leading dancers at the Opera-house.

The consequence is, when a young lady rises to dance, we no longer see the graceful, easy step of the gentlewoman, but the laboured, and often indelicate exhibitions of the posture-mistress.—Dances from *ballets* are introduced; and instead of the jocund and beautifully-organized movements of hilarity in concord, we are shocked by the most extravagant theatrical imitations. The chaste minuet is banished; and, in place of dignity and grace, we behold strange wheelings on one leg; stretching out the other till our eye meets the garter; and a variety of endless contortions, fitter for the zenana of an eastern satrap, or the gardens of Mahomet, than the ball-room of an Englishwoman of quality and virtue.

These *ballet* dances are, we now see, generally attempted. I say *attempted*, for not one young woman in five hundred can, from the very nature of the thing, after all her study, perform them better than could be done any day by the commonest *figurante* on the stage. We all know, that, to be a fine opera-dancer, requires unremitting practice, and a certain disciplining of the limbs, which hardly any private gentlewoman would consent to undergo. Hence, ladies can never hope to arrive

at any comparison with even the poorest public professor of the art; and therefore, to attempt the extravagancies of it, is as absurd
as it is indelicate.

The utmost in dancing to which a gentlewoman ought to aspire, is an agile and graceful movement of her feet, an harmonious motion with her arms, and a corresponding easy
carriage of her whole body. But, when she
has gained this proficiency, should she find
herself so unusually mistress of the art as to
be able, in any way, to rival the professors
by whom she has been taught, she must ever
hold in mind, that *the same style of dancing is
not equally proper for all kinds of dances.*

For instance, the English country-dance
and the French cotillion require totally different movements. I know that it is a common thing to introduce all the varieties of
opera-steps into the simple figure of the former. This ill-judged fashion is inconsistent
with the character of the dance, and, consequently, so destroys the effect, that no pleasure is produced to the eye of the judicious
spectator by so discordant an exhibition.

The characteristic of an English country-dance is that of *gay simplicity*. The steps should be few and easy ; and the corresponding motion of the arms and body unaffected, modest, and graceful.

Before I go farther on the subject, I cannot but stop a little to dwell, more particularly, on the necessity there is for more attention than we usually find paid to the management of the arms and general person in dancing.

In looking on at a ball, perhaps you will see that every woman, in a dance of twenty couple, moves her feet with sufficient atten-tion to beauty aed elegance ; but, with regard to the deportment of the rest of the person, most likely you will not discover one in a hundred who seems to know more about it than the most uncultivated damsel that ever jogged at a village wake.

I cannot exactly describe what it is that we see in the carriage of our young ladies in the dance; for it is difficult to point out a want by any other expression than a negative : but it is only requisite for my readers to recal to memory the many inanimate, ungraceful forms, from the waist upwards, that they nightly see at balls, and I need not describe more circumstantially.

For these ladies to suppose that they are fine dancers, because they execute a variety of difficult steps with ease and precision, is a great mistake. The motion of the feet is but half the art of dancing: the other, and indeed the most conspicuous part, lies in the movement of the body, arms, and head. Here elegance must be conspicuous.

The body should always be poised with such ease, as to command a power of graceful undulation, in harmony with the motion of the limbs in the dance. Nothing is more ugly than a stiff body and neck, during this lively exercise. The general carriage should be elevated and light; the chest thrown out, the head easily erect, but flexible to move with every turn of the figure; and the limbs should be all braced and animated with the spirit of motion, which seems ready to bound through the very air. By this elasticity pervading the whole person, when the dancer moves off, her flexile shape will gracefully sway with the varied steps of her feet; and her arms, instead of hanging loosely by her side, or rising abruptly and squarely up, to take hands with her partner, will be raised in beautiful and harmonious unison and time with the music and the figure; and her whole person will thus exhibit, to the delighted eye, perfection in beauty, grace, and motion.

This attention to the movement of the general figure, and particularly to that of the arms (for with them is the charm of elegant action), though in a moderated degree, is equally applicable to the English country-dance and the Scotch reel, as to the minuet, the cotillion, and other French dances.

A general idea of general grace, in all dances, being laid down as a first principle in this elegant art, I shall suggest a few remarks on the leading characters of each style; and from them, I hope, my fair friends will be able to gather some rules which may serve them as useful auxiliaries to the lessons of their dancing-master.

The English country-dance, as its very name implies, consists of simplicity and cheerfulness; hence the female, who engages in it, must aim at nothing more, in treading its easy mazes, than executing a few simple steps with unaffected elegance. Her body, her arms, the turn of her head, the expression of her countenance, all must bear the same character of negligent grace, of elegant activity, of decorous gaiety.

The Scotch reel has steps appropriated to itself, and in the dance can never be displaced for those of France, without an absurdity too ridiculous to even imagine without laughing. There are no dancers in the world more expressive of inward hilarity and happiness than the Scotch are, when performing in their own reels. The music is sufficient (so jocund are its sounds) to set a whole company on their feet in a moment, and to dance with all their might till it ceases, like people bit by the tarantula. Hence, as the character of reels is merriment, they must be performed with much more *joyance* of manner than even the country-dance; and therefore they are better adapted (as society is now constituted) to the social private circle than to the public ball. They demand a frankness of deportment, an undisguised jocularity, which few large parties will properly admit; therefore they are more at home in the baronial and kindred-filled hall of the thane of the Highland clan, than in the splendid and mixed ball-room of the now modish Anglo-Scottish earl.

French dances, which include minuets, cotillions, and all the round of *ballet* figures, admit of every new refinement and dexterity in the agile art; and while exhibiting in them, there is no step, no turn, no attitude within the verge of maiden delicacy that the dancer may not adopt and practise.

I must acknowledge, that there is something in the harmonious and undulating movements of the minuet particularly pleasing to my idea of female grace and dignity; and I remember seeing her Highness, the Princess de P———, at the court of Naples, go through the *Menuet de la Cour* with so eminent a degree of enchanting elegance, that there was not a person present who was not in raptures with her deportment.

The young Arch-Duke C——, of A——,
was then a youth, and an incognito visitant
with the Prince de V—— F——, and he
was so charmed with the dancing of her
Highness (whose partner was the renowned
General Marchese di M—— ;) that, in his
own heroic manner, he exclaimed to me, who
then sat by his side,—" Ah! Madame, that is
more interesting than even the Pyrrhic dance !
it reminds me of the beautiful movement of
the sun and moon in the heavens !"

The *minuet* is now almost out of fashion ;
but we yet have its serious movements in
many of the dances adopted from the French
ballet; and in these every gradation of grace,
and, if I may say it, sentiment in action, may
be discovered. The rapid changes of the cotillion are admirably calculated for the display of elegant gaiety; and I hope, that their
animated evolvements will long continue a favourite accomplishment and amusement with
our youthful fair.

Though much of graceful display is made
in these dances, yet there are many rivals in
the cotillion contending for the palm of su-

periority; and the contest throughout, if maintained with the original elegant decorum of the design, may be continued with undeviating modesty and discretion.

But with regard to the lately-introduced German waltz, I cannot speak so favourably. I must agree with Goetté, when writing of the national dance of his country, " that none but husbands and wives can with any propriety be partners in the waltz."

There is something in the close approximation of persons, in the attitudes, and in the motion, which ill agrees with the delicacy of woman, should she be placed in such a situation with any other man than the most intimate connection she can have in life. Indeed, I have often heard men, of no very overstrained feeling, say, " that there are very few women in the world with whom they could bear to dance the German waltz."

The fandango, though graceful in its own country, (because danced from custom with as reserved a mind as our maidens would make a courtesy,) is, nevertheless, when attempted here, too great a display of the person for any

modest Englishwoman to venture. It is a *solo!*
Imagine what must be the assurance of the
young woman, who, unaccustomed by the
habits of her country to such singular exhibitions of herself, could get up in a room full
of company, and, with an unblushing face, go
through all the evolutions, postures, and
vaultings of the Spanish fandango? Certainly there are few discreet men in England
who would say, " such a woman I should like
for my wife !"

The castanets, which are used in this dance,
by attracting extraordinary attention, afford
another argument against its being adopted
any where but on the stage. The tam-
bourin, the cymbals, and all other noisy ac-
companiments, in the hands of a lady-dancer,
are equally blameable ; and though a woman
may, by their means exhibit her agility and
person to advantage, she may depend on it,
that, while the artist only is admired, the woman will sink into contempt ; and that,
though she may possibly meet with lovers to
throw a score of embroidered handkerchiefs at
her feet, she will hardly encounter one of a

thousand who will venture to trust himself to the offering her the bond of a single gold ring.

The bullero, another of our Spanish importations, is a dance of so questionable a description, that I cannot but proscribe it also. It may be performed with perfect modesty; but the sentiment of it depends so entirely on the disposition of the dancer, that Delicacy dare hardly venture to inrol herself in its lists, lest the partner chosen for her might be of a temper to turn its gaiety into licentiousness; to produce blushes of shame where she promised herself the glow of pleasure, and send her away, from what ought to have been an innocent amusement, filled with the bitterness of insulted delicacy.

In short, in addressing my fair countrywomen on this subject, I would sum up my advice, in regard to the choice of dances, by warning them against the introduction of new-fangled fashions of this sort. Let them leave the languishing and meretricious attitudes of modern *ballet* teachers to the dancing-girls of India, or to the Circassian slaves of Turkey, whose disgraceful business is to please a tyrant, for whom they can feel no love.

Let our British fair also turn away from the almost equally unchaste dances of the southern kingdoms of the continent; and, content with the gay step of France and the active merriment of Scotland, with their own festive movements, continue their native country balls to their blameless delight, and to the gratification of every tasteful and benevolent observer.

While thus remarking on the manner of dancing, it may not be unacceptable to add a few words on the dress most appropriate to its light and unembarrassed motions.

Long trains are, of course, too cumbrous an appendage to be intentionally assumed when proposing to dance; but it must also be remarked, that very short petticoats are as inelegant as the others are inconvenient. Scanty, circumscribed habiliments impede the action of the limbs, and, besides their indelicacy, show the leg in the least graceful of all possible points of view. The most elegant attire for a ball, is, that the under garments should be absolutely short, but the upper one (which should be of light material) should reach at least to the top of the instep : it should also be sufficiently full to fall easily in folds from the waist downwards to the foot. By this arrangement, when the dancer begins her graceful exercise, the drapery will elegantly adapt itself to the motion and contour of her limbs; and falling accidently on her foot, or as accidently, when she bounds along, discovering, under its flying folds, her beautifully-turned ancle,—symmetry and grace will be occasionally displayed almost unconsciously ; and thus Modesty, taken unawares, will adorn, with her blushes, the perfect lineaments of female beauty.

What has been said in behalf of simple and appropriate dancing, may also be whispered in the ear of the fair practioner in music ; and, by analogy, she may, not unbeneficially, apply the suggestions to her own case.

There are many young women, who, when they sit down to the piano or the harp, or to sing, twist themselves into so many contor-

tions, and writhe their bodies and faces about
into such actions and grimaces, as would almost incline one to believe that they are suf-
fering under the torture of the tooth-ach or the
gout. Their bosoms heave, their shoulders
shrug, their heads swing to the right and left,
their lips quiver, their eyes roll; they sigh,
they pant, they seem ready to expire! And
what is all this about? They are merely
playing a favourite concerto, or singing a
new Italian song.

If it were possible for these conceit-in-
toxicated warblers, these languishing dolls, to
guess what rational spectators say of their
follies, they would be ready to break their instruments and be dumb for ever. What they
call *expression in singing,* at the rate they
would show it, is only fit to be exhibited on
the stage, when the character of the song
intends to portray the utmost ecstasy of
passion to a sighing swain. In short, such
an echo to the words and music of a love-
ditty is very improper in any young woman
who would wish to be thought as pure in
heart as in person. If amatory addresses are

to be sung, let the expression be in the voice and the composition of the air, not in the looks and gestures of the lady-singer. The utmost that she ought to allow herself to do, when thus breathing out the accents of love, is to wear a serious, tender countenance. More than this is bad, and may produce reflections in the minds of the hearers very inimical to the reputation of the fair warbler.

While touching on song, it may not be un-welcome to my truly virgin readers, to have their own delicate rejections sanctioned by a matron's judgment against a horde of amorous legends, now chanted forth in almost every assembly where they put their heads. Pretty music and elegant poetry seem sufficient ex-cuses to obtain, in these days, not only pardon, but approbation, for the most exceptionable verses that can fall from the pen of man. Such madrigals are now sung with equal ap-plause by mother and daughter, chaste and unchaste; all unite in shamelessly breathing forth words (and with appropriate languish-ments too) which hardly would become the lips of a Thais! Libertines may feel pleasure in such exhibitions, men of principle must turn away disgusted.

Set, then, this music of Paphos far aside; instead of songs of wantons, if we are to have amatory odes, let us listen to the chaste pleadings of a Petrarch, to the mutual vows of virtuous attachment My young friend may then sing with downcast eyes and timid voice; but no blush needs to stain her cheek, no thrill of shame shake her bosom. She merely chants of nature's feelings; and, Modesty veiling the sensibility she describes, angels might hearken and be pleased.

By this slight sketch, my dear readers will perceive that I mean *simplicity* to be the principle and the decoration of all their actions, as it should pervade them in the dance, so it should imbue their voice and action in playing and in singing.

Let their attitude at the piano, or the harp, be easy and graceful. I strongly exhort them to avoid a stiff, awkward, elbowing position at either; but they must observe an elegant flow of figure at both. The latter certainly admits of most grace, as

the shape of the instrument is calculated, in
every respect, to show a fine figure to advantage. The contour of the whole form, the
turn and polish of a beautiful hand and arm,
the richly-slippered and well-made foot on the
pedal stops, the gentle motion of a lovely neck,
and, above all, the sweetly-tempered expression of an intelligent countenance; these are
shown at one glance, when the fair performer
is seated unaffectedly, yet gracefully, at the
harp.

Similar beauty of position may be seen in a
lady's management of a lute, a guittar, a mandolin, or a lyre. The attitude at a piano-
forte, or at a harpsichord, is not so happily
adapted to grace. From the shape of the instrument, the performer must sit directly in
front of a straight line of keys; and her own
posture being correspondingly erect and
square, it is hardly possible that it should not
appear rather inelegant. But if it attain not
the *ne plus ultra* of grace, at least she may
prevent an air of stiffness; she may move her
hands easily on the keys, and bear her head
with that elegance of carriage which cannot

fail to impart its own character to the whole
of her figure. One of the most graceful forms
that I ever saw sit at an instrument, is that of
St. Cecilia, painted by Sir Joshua Reynolds, playing on the organ. It is the portrait of the late Mrs. R. B. Sheridan; and,
from the simplicity of the attitude and the
graceful elevation of the head, it is, without
exception, one of the most interesting pictures
I ever beheld. A living instance of all what
beauty and grace, elegance and propriety
combined can do, has always been admired
in the Marchioness of D———— by all
those who ever had the felicity to see and
hear her at the piano; an engraving of her
portrait, in that attitude, would teach every
female lover of the art unaffected elegance,
much more effectually than all what the ad-
vices and ability of masters can ever be able
to perform.

If ladies, in meditating on grace of deportment, would rather consult the statues of fine
sculptors, and the figures of excellent pain-
ters, than the lessons of their dancing-masters,
or the dictates of their looking-glasses, we

should, doubtless, see simplicity where we now find affectation, and a thousand ineffable graces taking place of the present *regime* of absurdity and conceit.

It was by studying the perfect sculpture of Greece and Rome, that a certain lady of rank, eminent for her peculiarly beautiful attitudes, acquired so great a superiority in mien above her fair cotemporaries of every court in which she became an inmate. It was by meditating on the classic pictures of Poussin, that one of the first tragic actresses, on the French stage, learnt to move and look like the *daughter of the sun.* And by a similar study has our own Melpomene caught inspiration from the pencil of Correggio and Rubens.

Glancing at the graphic art, reminds me that some degree of proficiency in this interesting accomplishment is also an object of study with my fair young countrywomen. I shall not make any observation on their progress in the art itself, only with regard to their manner of practising it.

Both for health and beauty's sake, they should be careful not to stoop too much, or to

sit too long in the exercise of the pencil. A
bending position of the chest and head, when
frequently assumed, is apt to contract the
lungs, round the back, redden the face, and give
painful digestions and head-ach. An awkward
posture in writing, reading, or sewing, is pro-
ductive of the same bad effects; and what may
seem almost incredible, (but many who have
witnessed the same, can, I am sure, give their
evidence in support of my representation)
there are young persons, who, when writing,
drawing, reading, or working, keep a sort of
ludicrous time with their occupation, by making a succession of unmeaning and hideous
grimaces. I have seen a pretty young woman,
while writing a letter to her lover, draw up her
lips, and twist the muscles of her face in every
direction that her pen moved ; and so ugly
did she look during this sympathetic performance, that I could not forbear thinking
that, could her swain see the object then dic-
tating her vows, he would take fright at the
metamorphosis, and never be made to believe
it could be the same person.

Mumbling to yourself, while reading, is also

another very inelegant habit. A person should either read determinately so much aloud as to be heard distinctly by the company present, or peruse her book so completely to herself as not even to move her lips. An inward muttering, or a silent motion of the mouth, while reading, is equally unpleasant to the observer, and disfiguring to the observed.

In short, there is nothing, however minute in manners, however insignificant in appearance, that does not demand some portion of attention from a well-bred and highly-polished young woman. An author of no small literary renown, has observed that several of the minutest habits or acts of some individuals, may give sufficient reasons to guess at their temper. The choice of a gown, or even the folding and sealing of a letter, will bespeak the shrew and the scold, the careless and the negligent. This observation I have made myself, not only in this, but in several other countries. The Marchioness of B—— addressed me, a few years ago, in a letter so cleanly folded, so carefully sealed, that I was really prejudiced in her favour, ere

I saw that my surmises were right; and the
flame-colour ribbon, fluttering about the Hon.
Mrs. D's head had given me a foreboding of
her acrimonious and fiery disposition. These
fine and almost imperceptible objects are the
touches which bring the whole to its utmost
perfection. They are the varnish to the picture, the polish to the gem, the points to the
diamond.

I will go farther upon this subject. The
very voice of an individual, the tone she assumes in speaking to strangers, or even familiarly to her friends, will lead a keen observer
to discover what elements her temper is made
of. The low key belongs to the sullen, sulky,
obstinate; the shrill note, to the petulant, the
pert, the impatient; some will pronounce the
common and trite question, " how *do* you *do ?*"
with such harshness and raucity, that they
seem positively angry with you that you should
ever *do* at all. Some affect a lispingness,
which at once betrays childishness and down-
right nonsense; others will bid their words
to gallop so swiftly, that the ablest ear is unable to follow the rapid race, and gathers nothing

but confused and unmeaning sounds. All these extremes are to be avoided; and, although nature has differently formed the organs of speech for different individuals, yet there is a mode to correct nature's own aberrations. I have heard of sensible men who, merely for the tone of voice which did not quite harmonize with their ears, have dropped the connection with women who, in all other points, were unexceptionable.

Admit this, and another salutary truth will be made manifest. If good breeding and graceful refinement are ever *most proper*, they are always so. It is not sufficient that Amaryllis is amiable and elegant in her whole deportment to strangers and to her acquaintance; she must be undeviatingly so to her most intimate friends, to nearest relations, to father, mother, brothers, sisters, husband. She must have no *dishabille* for them, either of mind or person.

This last word inclines me to pursue the hint farther; to exhort my fair readers, while I plead for consistency in manners, also to carry the analogy to dress. If they would always appear amiable, elegant, and endearing to the beings with whom they are to spend their lives, let them always make those beings the first objects of their accomplishments, their manners, and their dress. Let them never appear before these tender relatives in the disgusting negligence of disordered and soiled clothes. By this has many a lovely girl lost her lover; and by this, has many an amiable wife alienated the affections of her husband.

Let me then, in concluding this chapter, again repeat, that consistency is the soul of female power, the charm of her fascination, the bond of her social happiness.

CONTINUATION OF THE SAME SUBJECT.

THE carriage of a woman to her equals being
founded on a just appreciation of their merits,
and a proper respect to herself, the same sentiment will be found to pervade her conduct to
her superiors in rank.

With regard to men, when they occupy a
higher station than herself, she must proportion
reverential courtesy to them according to the
rules of court ceremony. If she knows them
merely as officers high in authority under the
king, or as nobles distinguished by his honours;
her manner must then be that of calm, dignified
respect. But when she finds that merit is yet
higher in any of these men than his titles,
then, let her show the homage of the soul, as
well as that of the body; for real greatness
ennobles the head which bows.

With regard to her own sex, the same rule
must be observed. There are certain regula-
tions in society which are called Laws of Precedence. They are of as much use in main-

taining a due and harmonious order amongst
civilized men and women, as the law of attraction is to preserve the heavenly bodies in
their proper orbits. As one star differs from
another in magnitude and splendor, in proportion to the destiny it hath to fulfil ; so do
the talents and degrees of men vary according
to the allotted duties they have to perform.
Hence, as in astronomy, we think not of de-
spising Mercury, because he is not as large as
Saturn, nor of speaking of our own earth as a
planet of no account, because she has not four
moons like Jupiter; so, in parity of reasoning,
we do not esteem our inferiors, or equals, the
less, because they do not fill the first orders in
society. All ranks have their proper place,
the station in which they can be the most
useful; and it is in proportion as they perform
their respective duties that we must respect the
individuals.

We therefore regard society as a grand ma-
chine, in which each member has the place
best fitted for him; or, to make use of a more
common illustration, as a vast drama, in which
every person has the part allotted to him most

appropriate to his abilities. One enacts the King, others the Lords, others the Commons; but all obey the Great Director, who best knows what is in man. Regarding things in this light, all arrogance, all pride, all envyings and contempt of others, from their relative degrees, disappear, as emotions to which we have no pretensions. We neither endowed ourselves with high birth or eminent talents. We are altogether beings of a creation independent of our own will; and, therefore, bearing our own honours as a gift, not as a right, we shall condescend to our inferiors, (whose place it might have been our lot to fill) and regard with deference our superiors, whom Heaven, by so elevating them, intended we should respect.

This sentiment of order in the mind, this conviction of the beautiful harmony in a well-organized civil society, gives us dignity with our inferiors, without allaying it with the smallest particle of pride; by keeping them at a due distance, we merely maintain ourselves and them in the rank in which a higher Power has placed us; and the condescension of our

general manners to them, and our kindnesses
in their exigencies, and generous approbation
of their worth, are sufficient acknowledge-
ments of sympathy, to show that we avow the
same nature with themselves, the same origin,
the same probation, the same end.

Our demeanour with our equals is more a
matter of policy. To be indiscreetly familiar,
to allow of liberties being taken with your
good-nature; all this is likely to happen with
people of the same rank with ourselves, unless we hold our mere acquaintance at a proper distance, by a certain reserve. A woman
may be gay, ingenuous, perfectly amiable to
her associates, and yet reserved. Avoid all
sudden intimacies, all needless secret-telling,
all closeting about nonsense, caballing, taking
mutual liberties with each other in regard to
domestic arrangements: in short, beware of
familiarity! The kind of familiarity which
is common in families, and amongst women
of the same classes in society, is that of an indiscriminate gossiping; an interchange of
thoughts without any effusion of the heart.
Then an unceremonious way of reproach-

ing each other, for a real or supposed
neglect; a coarse manner of declaring your
faults; a habit of jangling on trifles; a habit
of preferring your own whims or ease before
that of the persons about you: an indelicate
way of breaking into each other's privacy. In
short, doing every thing that declares the total
oblivion of all politeness and decent manners.

This series of errors happens, every day
amongst brothers and sisters, husbands and
wives, and female acquaintances: and what
are the consequences? Distaste, disgust, ever-
lasting quarrels, and perhaps a total rupture in
the end!

I have seen many families bound together
by the tenderest affection; I have seen many
hearts wrought into each other by the sweet
amalgamation of friendship: but with none
did I ever find this delicious foretaste of the
society in Elysium, where a never-failing politeness was not mingled in all their thoughts,
words, and actions to each other.

Deportment to superiors must ever carry
with it that peculiar degree of ceremony
which their rank demands. No intimacy of

intercourse with them, no friendship and affection from them, ought ever to make us forget the certain respect which their stations require. Thus, for a mere gentlewoman to think of arrogating to herself the same homage of courtesy that is paid to a lady of quality, or to deny the just tribute of precedence, in every respect, to that lady, would be as absurd as presumptuous. Yet we see it; and ridicule from the higher circles is all she derives from her vain pretensions. By the same rule, every woman of rank must yield due courtesy to those above her, in the just gradation, according to their elevation in the scale of nobility. The law of courts on this subject is soon understood, and, as a guide to my young readers, who may not yet have been sufficiently informed, I shall, beneath, give them a list of female titles, according to their precedence in the march of hereditary and other honours. I shall begin with the highest rank, as it is that which, in all public processions, or in private parties, has the right of standing or moving first.

As the crown of the whole, I set down a

Queen. Then Princesses. Then follow, in regular order, Duchesses, Marchionesses, Countesses. The Wives of the Eldest sons of Marquisses. The Wives of the Younger sons of Dukes. Daughters of Dukes. Daughters of Marquisses. Viscountesses. Wives of the eldest sons of Earls. Daughters of Earls. Wives of the younger sons of Marquisses. Baronesses. Wives of the eldest sons of Viscounts. Daughters of Viscounts. Wives of the younger sons of Earls. Wives of the eldest sons of Barons. Daughters of Barons. Wives of the younger sons of Viscounts. Wives of the younger sons of Barons. Wives of Baronets. Wives of Privy Counsellors, Commoners. Wives of Judges. Wives of Knights of the Garter. Wives of Knights of the Bath. Wives of Knights of the Thistle. Wives of Knights Bachelors. Wives of Generals. Wives of Admirals. Wives of the eldest sons of Baronets. Daughters of Knights according to their fathers' precedence. Wives of the younger sons of Baronets. Wives of Esquires and Gentlemen. Daughters of Esquires and Gentlemen. Wives of Citizens and Burgesses. The Wives of Military and Naval Officers of course take precedence of each other in correspondence with the rank of their husbands.

This scale, if every young lady would bear in mind and conform to it, is a sufficient guide to the mere ceremony of precedence ; and would effectually prevent those dangerous disputes in ball-rooms about places, and those rude jostlings in going in and out of assemblies, which are not more disagreeable than ill-bred. It is the perfection of fine breeding to know your place, to be acquainted with that of others ; and to fall gracefully into your station accordingly. While the gentlewoman is content to move in the train of female honours, the dignified decorum of step forms one graceful link in the chain of society; but if she struggles to get before, strikes one to her right and the other to her left; treads down alike her equals and her superiors, in her eagerness for pre-eminence; we fly from the shrew, and declare her unworthy of fellowship with any degree of well-ordered females.

The deference we pay to superiors, our inferiors will refund to us ; and, therefore, if we wish to maintain " that proud submission, that dignified obedience," which binds the subject, through various gradations, to the sovereign, we must teach our untractable spirits to bend to the cogent reasons and salutary ordinances of high authority.

Women in every country have a greater influence than men chose to confess. Though haughtiness of mind will not allow them always to acknowledge the truth, yet we see the proof in its effects ; and, in consequence, must exhort women, by yielding their deference to the laws of honorary precedence, to teach men to obey them ; and, rather to emulate such distinctions, than seek to pull down the possessors to the level of the common herd.

CONCLUSION.

WHEN so much has been said of the body
and its accoutrements, I cannot but subjoin a
few words on the intelligence which animates
the frame, and of the organ which imparts its
meaning.

Connected speech is granted to mankind
alone. Parrots may prate and monkeys chat-
ter, but it is only to the reasonable being that
power of combining ideas, expressing their
import, and uttering, in audible sounds, in all
its various gradations, the language of sense
and judgment, of love and resentment, is
awarded as a gift, that gives us a proud and
undeniable superiority above all the rest of
the creation.

To employ this faculty well and gracefully,
is one grand object of education. The mere
organ itself, as to sound, is like a musical instrument, to be modulated with elegance, or
struck with the disorderly nerve of coarseness
and vulgarity.

I must add to what has been said before, on

the subject, that excessive rapidity of speaking is, in general, even with a clear enunciation, very disagreeable; but, when it is accompanied with a shrill voice, high in alt, the effect is then inexpressibly discordant and hideous. The first orator the heathen world knew, so far remedied the natural defects of his speech, (and they were the most embarrassing) as to become the most easy and persuasive of speakers. In like manner, when a young woman finds any difficulty or inelegance in her organs, she ought to pay the strictest attention to rectify the fault.

Should she have too quick or encumbered an articulation, she ought to read with extreme slowness, for several hours in the day, and even pay attention in speaking to check the rapidity or confusion of her utterance. By similar antidotal means, she must attack a propensity of talking in a high key. Better err in the opposite extreme, while she is prosecuting her cure, as the voice will gradually and imperceptibly attain its most harmonious pitch; than, by at first attempting the medium, most likely, retain too much of the screaming key.

A clear articulation, a tempered intonation, and in a moderate key, are essentials in the voice of an accomplished female. For her graceful peculiarities, those nature and rare taste must bestow. Fine judgment and delicate sensibility are the best schoolmistresses on this subject. Indeed, where is it that, in relation to man or woman, we shall find, that an improved understanding, an enlightened mind, and a refined taste, are not the best polishers of manners, and in all respects the most efficient handmaids of the Muses?

Let me then, in one short sentence, in one tender adieu, my fair readers and endeared friends! enforce upon your minds, that if Beauty be woman's weapon, it must be feathered by the Graces, pointed by the eye of Discretion, and shot by the hand of Virtue!

Look then, my sweet pupils, not merely to your mirrors, when you would decorate yourselves for conquest, but consult the *speculum*, which will reflect your hearts and minds. Remember that it is the affections of a sensible and reasonable soul you hope to subdue, and seek for arms likely to carry the fortress.

He that is worthy, must love answering excellence. Which of you all would wish to
marry a man merely for the colour of his eye,
or the shape of his leg ? Think not then worse
of him than you would do of yourselves ; and,
hope not to satisfy his better wishes with the
possession of a merely handsome wife.

Beauty of person will ever be found a dead
letter, unless it be animated with beauty of
mind. We must then, not only cultivate the
shape, the complexion, the air, the attire, the
manners ; but most assiduously must our attention be devoted to teach " the young idea how
to shoot," and to fashion the unfolding mind
to judgment and virtue. By such culture, it
will not be merely the charming girl, the cap-
tivating woman we shall present to the world ;
but, the dutiful daughter, affectionate sister,
tender wife, judicious mother, faithful friend,
and amiable acquaintance.

Let these then be the fair images which will
form themselves on the models drawn by my
not inexperienced pen ! Let me see Beauty,
whose soul is Virtue, approach me with the
chastened step of Modesty ; and, ere she ad-

vances from behind the heavenly cloud that envelops her, I shall behold Love and all the Graces hovering in air to adorn and attend her charms!

This may be thy picture, lovely daughter of Albion! Make thyself then worthy of the likeness, and thou wilt fulfil the fondest wish of thine unknown friend.

THE END.

RECIPES.

RECIPES.

Paste of Palermo.

[This paste for the hands, to use instead of soap, preserves them from chopping, smooths their surface, and renders them soft.]

Take a pound of soft soap, half a pint of sallad oil, the same quantity of spirits of wine, the juice of three lemons, a little silver sand, and a sufficient quantity of what perfume pleases the sense. The oil and soap must be first boiled together in an earthen pipkin. The other ingredients to be added after boiling; and, when cool, amalgamate into a paste with the hands.

Fard.

[This useful paste is good for taking off sun-
burnings, effects of weather on the face, and
accidental cutaneous eruptions. It must be
applied at going to bed. First wash the
face with its usual ablution, and when dry,
rub this fard all over it, and go to rest with
it on the skin. This is excellent for almost
constant use.]

Take two ounces of oil of sweet almonds,
ditto of spermaceti : melt them in a pipkin
over a slow fire. When they are dissolved
and mixed, take it off the fire, and stir into it
one table-spoonful of fine honey. Continue
stirring till it is cold ; and then it is fit for
use.

Lip Salve.

A quarter of a pound of hard marrow, from
the marrow-bone. Melt it over a slow fire, as
it dissolves gradually, pour the liquid marrow
into an earthern pipkin, then add to it an
ounce of spermaceti, twenty raisins of the sun,
stoned, and a small portion of alcanna root,

sufficient to colour it a bright vermilion. Simmer these ingredients over a slow fire for ten minutes, then strain the whole through muslin; and while hot, stir into it one tea-spoonful of the balsam of Peru. Pour it into the boxes in which it is to remain; it will there stiffen, and become fit for use.

Lavender Water.

Take of rectified spirits of wine half a pint, essential oil of lavender two drachms, otto of roses five drops. Mix all together in a bottle, and cork it for use.

Unction de Maintenon.

[The use of this is to remove freckles. The mode of application is this. Wash the face at night with elder-flower water, then anoint it with the unction. In the morning cleanse your skin from its oily adhesion, by washing it copiously in rose water.]

Take of Venice soap an ounce, dissolve it in half an ounce of lemon juice, to which add of oil of bitter almonds and deliquated oil of tar-

tar, each a quarter of an ounce. Let the
mixture be placed in the sun till it acquires the
consistence of ointment. When in this
state, add three drops of the oil of rhodium,
and keep it for use.

———

Crême de l'Enclos.

[This is an excellent wash, to be used night
and morning for the removal of tan.]

Take half a pint of milk, with the juice of
a lemon, and a spoonful of white brandy, boil
the whole, and skim it clear from all skum.
When cool, it is ready for use.

———

Pommade de Seville.

[This simple application is much in request
with the Spanish ladies, for taking off the
effects of the sun, and to render the complexion brilliant.]

Take equal parts of lemon juice and white
of eggs. Beat the whole together in a var-
nished earthen pipkin, and set on a slow fire.
Stir the fluid with a wooden spoon till it has

acquired the consistence of soft pomatum. Perfume it with some sweet essence, and, before you apply it, carefully wash the face with rice water.

———◆———

Baume à l'Antique.

[This is a very fine cure for chopped lips.]

Take four ounces of the oil of roses, half an ounce of white wax, and half an ounce of spermaceti; melt them in a glass vessel, and stir them with a wooden spoon, pour it out into glass-cups for use.

———◆———

Wash for the Hair.

[This is a cleanser and brightener of the head and hair, and should be applied in the morning.]

Beat up the whites of six eggs into a froth, and with that anoint the head close to the roots of the hair. Leave it to dry on; then wash the head and hair thoroughly with a mixture of rum and rose-water in equal quantities.

Aura and Cephalus.

[This curious receipt is of Grecian origin, as
its name plainly indicates, and is said to
have been very efficacious in preventing or
even removing premature wrinkles from the
face of the Athenian fair.]

Put some powder of the best myrrh upon
an iron plate, sufficiently heated to melt the
gum gently, and when it liquifies, hold your
face over it, at a proper distance to receive the
fumes without inconvenience; and, that you
may reap the whole benefit of the fumigation,
cover your head with a napkin. It must be
observed, however, that if the applicant feels
any head-ach, she must desist, as the remedy
will not suit her constitution, and ill consequences might possibly ensue.

Madame Recamier's Pommade.

[This was communicated by this lady as being
used in France and Italy, by those who pro-
fessionally, or by choice, are engaged in
exercises which require long and great ex-

ertions of the limbs, as dancing, playing on instruments, &c.]

Take any suitable quantity ot *Axungia Cervi*, i. e. the fat of a red stag or hart; add to it the same quantity of olive oil, (Florence oil is preferable to any of the kind,) and half the quantity of virgin wax; melt the whole in an earthen vessel, well-glazed, over a slow fire, and, when properly mixed, leave it to cool.— This ointment has been applied also with considerable efficacy in cases of rheumatism.

———

A Wash for the Face.
This receip is well known in France, and much extolled by the ladies of that country as efficacious and harmless.]

Take equal parts of the seeds of the melon, pompion, gourd, and cucumber, pounded and reduced to powder or meal; add to it fresh cream, sufficient to dilute the flour; beat all up together, adding a sufficient quantity of

milk, as it may be required, to make an ointment, and then apply it to the face: leave it
there for half an hour, and then wash it off
with warm soft water.

———

A Paste for the Skin.

[This may be recommended in cases when
the skin seems to get too loosely attached
to the muscles.]

Boil the whites of four eggs in rose water,
add to it a sufficient quantity of alum; beat
the whole together till it takes the consistence
of a paste. This will give, when applied,
great firmness to the skin.

———

A Wash to give Lustre to the Face.

Infuse wheat-bran well-sifted, for three or
four hours in white wine vinegar; add to it
five yolks of eggs and a grain or two of ambergris, and distil the whole. When the bot-

tle is carefully corked, keep it for 12 or 15 days before you make use of it.

Pimpernel Water.

Pimpernel is a most wholesome plant, and often used on the continent for the purpose of whitening the complexion: it is there in so high reputation, that it is said generally, that it ought to be continually on the toilet of every lady who cares for the brightness of her skin.

Eau de Veau.

Boil a calf's foot in four quarts of river water till it is reduced to half the quantity. Add half a pound of rice, and boil it with crumb of white bread steeped in milk, a pound of fresh butter, and the whites of five fresh eggs; mix with them a small quantity of camphor and alum, and distil the whole. This receipt may be strongly recommended;

it is most beneficial to the skin, which it lubri-
cates and softens to a very comfortable degree.
The best manner of distilling these ingredients is in the *balneum mariæ;* that is in a bottle placed in boiling water.

———◆———

Rose Water.

Put some roses into water, add to them a
few drops of acid; the vitriolic acid seems to
be preferable to any—soon the water will assume both the colour and perfume of the
roses.

———◆———

Another.

Take two pounds of rose leaves, place them
on a napkin tied round the edges of a bason
filled with hot water, and put a dish of cold
water upon the leaves; keep the bottom water
hot, and change the water at top as soon as it
begins to grow warm; by this kind of distil-
lation you will extract a great quantity of the

essential oil of the roses by a process which cannot be expensive, and will prove very beneficial.

———

Virgin Milk.

A publication of this kind would certainly be looked upon as an imperfect performance, if we omitted to say a few words upon this famous cosmetic. It consists of a tincture of Benjoin, precipitated by water. The tincture of Benjoin is obtained by taking a certain quantity of that gum, pouring spirits of wine upon it, and boiling it till it becomes a rich tincture. If you pour a few drops of this tincture into a glass of water, it will produce a mixture which will assume all the appearance of milk, and retain a very agreeable perfume. If the face is washed with this mixture, it will, by calling the purple stream of the blood to the external fibres of the epidermis, produce on the cheeks a beautiful rosy colour; and, if left on the face to dry, it will render it clear and brilliant. It also removes

spots, freckles, pimples, erysipelatous eruptions, &c. &c. if they have not been of long
standing on the skin.

———

How to make Lavender Water.

Take four handfuls of dried lavender flow
ers, and sprinkle on them one quart of brandy,
the same quantity of white wine and rose-water; leave them to remain six days in a large
bottle well-corked up; let the liquor be distilled and poured off.

———

Sweet-scented Water.

[This agreeably-scented water is not only
a pleasant cosmetic, but also of great use in
nervous disorders.]

Put one quart of rose-water, and the same
quantity of orange-water, into a large and
wide-mouthed glass; strew upon it two handfuls of jessamine flowers, put the glass in the

balneum mariæ, or on a slow fire, and when it
is distilled, add to it a scruple of musk and
the same quantity of ambergris.

———◆———

Eau d'Ange.

Pound in a mortar fifteen cloves and one
pound of cinnamon, and put the whole into a
quart of water, with four grains of anniseed ;
let it stand over a charcoal fire twenty-four
hours, then strain off the liquor, and put it up
for use. This perfume is most excellent, and
will do well for the hands, face, and hair, to
which it communicates a very agreeable scent.

———◆———

Eau des Carmes.

[This water has been of a very long-standing
in repute with nearly every body on the
Continent ; it was invented by a Carmelite
Friar, as its name implies. It is of great
assistance in lowness of spirits, in rheumatic pains, and for the gout in the stomach.]

Take one quart of brandy, and infuse into it cinnamon, cloves, and angelica root, of each half an ounce ; coriander seeds, nutmegs grated, one ounce of each; a quarter of a pound of balm leaves, and two ounces of lemon peel; put the whole into a crucible, and let it stand near the fire three days; then mix with it one pint of balm water, and distil it over a slow fire ; drain off the liquor, and let it be well corked up in bottles for the space of one month before you make use of it.

Having given these beautifying Recipes, I shall add two or three, which only promise comfort.

Remedy for the Tooth-ach.

In two drachms of rectified spirits of wine dissolve one drachm of camphire, five grains of prepared opium, and ten drops of oil of box ; mix them well, and keep it well corked for use. If the pain arise from a hollow tooth, four or five drops on cotton to be put into the tooth ; or six or seven drops to be put on cotton into the ear on the side where the pain is felt. Should the patient not feel easier in a quarter of an hour, the same may be repeated. It has never failed on the second application.

An excellent Eye-water.

Take six ounces of rectified spirits of wine, dissolve in it one drachm of camphire, and half a pint of elder-flower water. Wash the eyes night and morning with this liquid ; it clears the vision, and strengthens the sight.

Corn Plaister,

Take one ounce of turpentine, half an ounce of red lead, one ounce of frankincense, half a pound of white rosin, one pint of Florence oil ; boil these ingredients in a pipkin, and keep stirring them over a slow fire with ar elder stick until it turns black ; then turn it out to harden for use. It must be applied by spreading it on a piece of leather oiled all over, and then put to the corn. Wearing it constantly for some time will effectually eradicate the corn.

———

To assuage the raging pain of a Corn by instant application.

Take equal parts of a roasted onion and soft soap, beat them up together, and apply them to the corn in a linen rag by way of poultice.

NOTES ON THE MIRROR OF THE GRACES.

In the elegant style which the Author of this treatise has adopted to delineate the fashions of the day,
as well as the general and invariable principles of taste
and judgment in adorning the fair, she could not help
making use of several expressions, the meaning of
which may not be obvious to all those who will find a
delight in perusing her book. The Editor, therefore,
has thought that a few explanatory notes would be of
advantage to all classes of readers, as they will, he
trusts, afford instruction to the young and inexperienced, and, at the same time, help the recollection of
past knowledge in those who might have in part forgotten the meaning of names in, and allusions to, ancient and modern history.

Page 22.—*Sacharissa.*] Lady Dorothy Sydney,
highly celebrated under this fictitious name by Wal-
ler, who, " a widower at the age of 25 years, felt for
her that tender passion which gave birth to verses that
made her beauty triumph over time. The Poet, however, not being so successful in his addresses to Sacharissa as he had been in the elegant strains with which
she had inspired him, her marriage with Lord Spencer,
Earl of Sunderland, was celebrated at Penhurst, on
the 20th of July, 1639." *Gallery of British Portraits.*

26. *The garb of childhood the foundation of a just pro-*

portion.] The eloquence of J. J. Rousseau, his deep
metaphysics, his numerous paradoxes would not have
recommended him to the notice of his cotemporaries
and of posterity, had it not been for the sound principles of education which he lays down in his
celebrated " Emile." He taught French mothers
their first duty, and wrenched the starving child from
the mercenary breath of the hired wet-nurse, to re-
place it on that bosom where nature had provided two
plentiful springs of ambrosial milk gushing there exclusively for the infant owner—he freed children from
the bandages of ridiculous custom, allowed them the
use of their growing limbs, and kept at a distance, for
ever, all the horrors of the rickets.

27. *Her, whose flying steps, &c.*] Camilla, Queen of
the Volsci, daughter of Metablus, was dedicated, when
young, to the service of Diana, and assisted Turnus
against Æneas. Virgil, of whose own creation this
personage seems to be, tells us that she was so swift
that she could run, or rather fly, over a field of corn,
without bending the blades, and make her way over the
sea without wetting her feet.

Last, from the Volscians, fair Camilla came,
And led her warlike troops, a warrior dame :
Unbred to spinning, in the loom unskill'd,
She chose the nobler Pallas of the field.
Mix'd with the first, the fierce Virago fought,
Sustain'd the toils of arms, the danger sought ;

Outstripp'd the winds in speed upon the plain ;
Flew o'er the fields, nor hurt the bearded grain :
She swept the seas, and, as she skimm'd along,
Her flying feet unbath'd on billows hung.

VIRGIL'S ÆNEIS, B. vii. 1094.

The same image is exhibited in " the Lady of the
Lake" in a new point of view and with much origin-
ality ;

> " What though no rule of courtly grace
> To measured mood had trained her pace ;
> A foot more light, a step more true,
> Ne'er from the heath-flower dashed the dew ;
> E'en the slight hare-bell raised its head
> Elastic from her airy tread.

Canto I. St. xviii.

P. 30. *Drapery of Co.*] Co, one of the Cyclades
Islands, in the Archipelago, noted for the very thin
drapery which the Coan ladies used to wear. How
could the father of physic, Hippocrates, who was born
there, bear to see his countrywomen so thinly clad, a
costume so injurious to their health ? There also
Apelles was born, and, perhaps his paintings contri-
buted to introduce the unwholesome fashion. However, it is worthy of remark that Praxiteles having
made two statues of Venus, one naked the other veiled ;
although the former was superior in beauty and perfection to the latter, the inhabitants of Co preferred
the clad one to the other

———— Video meliora proboque,

Deteriora sequor ———— ————   HORAT.

The Coan ladies generally dressed in white, and their
garments were so transparent, that the body could be
seen through them. They were hanged into cows, by
Venus. We should like to read in the Mythologists, that
it was as a punishment for their want of propriety and
decency ; but the reason assigned for so strange a metamorphosis is, that they favoured Hercules in one of
his labours.

P. 33. *Medea's cauldron.*] In order to revenge some
injuries which her husband's family had received from
Pelias, Medea advised his daughters to kill him and
boil his flesh in a cauldron, that he might, like Æson,
grow young again by the same process ; but she did
not apply the promised charm, and the body was con-
sumed by the heat of the fire.

P. 54. *Herse.*] Daughter of Cecrops, king of Athens,
beloved by Mercury. According to Ovid, she was un-
commonly beautiful ; for he says, in his usual hyper-
bolical style : " As much as the morning star exceeds
in brightness the other stars of Heaven, and as much
as the golden moon shines brighter than the morning
star, so much did Herse surpass all the other virgins
as she walked, an ornament to the solemnity and to
all the virgin train. *Medusa,* one of the three Gorgons,
who was metamorphosed so frightfully that the sight
of her face turned people into stones.

55. *The exquisitely fair complexion, c.*] The colour
of the hair generally agrees with that of the eyes and
eyebrows; yet we meet sometimes with beautiful young
women, who, to a fine outline of features and symmetry of parts, unite the peculiarity of blue eyes
with dark hair, or light hair with dark eyes, which
uncommon contrast gives a most expressive countenance, to those whom the fanciful hand of nature has
so formed. Struck with admiration at this curious
and pleasing accident, a modern poet says :

——————— FESTINA came
With sparkling *azure* eyes, with *ebon* hair,
And cheeks of *vermil* hue, a lovely fair;

69. *Plutus.*] Plutus, son of Jasius by Ceres, was
the God of Riches, and used to be represented blind,
lame, and with wings. Blind in allusion to the une-
qual distribution of riches in this world. Lame, because wealth is acquired slowly by industry. And
with wings, to show that, unless economy presides
over our actions, wealth will leave us with more velo-
city than it came.

72. *On the reverse, when no show of vanity.*] We may
apply here with great aptness and propriety, what
Tasso says of the rose-bud. " Quanto si mostra men
tanto è più bella." *Jerusal. Deliv.*

99. *Procrustean.*] Procrustes was a noted robber,
in that part of Attica called *Curdatus*, who measured

by his bed the travellers he had surprised and taken;
and, if too long for the fatal couch, cut them shorter,
but if too short, stretched them longer. *Vid. Ovid,
Met.* 7. 438.

102. *Thais.*] A famous courtezan of Athens, who
accompanied Alexander in his Asiatic conquests, and
gained such an ascendant over him, that she made
him burn the royal palace at Persepolis. Sir Joshua
Reynolds has left behind him a very fine specimen of
his talents in a painting of that subject.

151. *Phryne*] of Athens, mistress to Praxiteles, the
most renowned sculptor which that city ever produced.
She was so very handsome, that Apelles singled her
out as a model to paint his famous Venus Anadyomene.
She became very rich by the liberality of her lovers, and
made a proper use of her wealth. Another woman, of
that name, conquered the severity of her judges by unveiling her bosom before them; it must have happened when decency was so much the fashion, that no
prying eye could freely gaze upon that beautiful part
of a female's body—In ages much nearer our times,
the lavish exhibition of the bosom, (so much spoken
against in the foregoing pages) would have deprived
this theatrical trick of its effect.

165. *Sybaritical.*] Sybaris, a town of Calabria, so
well-known for the effeminacy of its inhabitants that
the word *Sybarite* became proverbial to designate a man
devoted to pleasure.

178. *Terpsıchore.*] The muse who presides over the art of dancing.

184. *Tarantula.*] A kind of spider, well-known in Italy, whose bite cannot be cured but by the exertion of jumping or dancing.

186. *Pyrrhic dance.*] This dance is said to have been invented by Pyrrhus the son of Achilles—It was performed by several men or women, and the figures were intended to represent the circumvolutions of the then-known planets around the sun.

J. Swan and Son, Printers, 76, Fleet Street, London.

Additional Illustrations

The Repository, London, 1814

La Belle assemblée, 1811

La Belle Assemblée, London, 1812

La Belle Assemblée, London, 1813

La Belle Assemblée, London, 1814

The Repository, London,   1816

The Repository, London,   1817

THE HANDBOOK OF PRACTICAL CUTTING
on the Centre Point System (1866) by Louis Devere

THE LADIES SELF-INSTRUCTOR in Millinery
& Mantua Making, Embroidery & Applique (1853)

THE LADIES' GUIDE TO NEEDLEWORK (1877)
by S. Annie Frost

THE LADIES HANDBOOK of Fancy & Ornamental Work
by Florence Hartley

LATE GEORGIAN COSTUME: The Tailor's
Friendly Instructor (1822) by J. Wyatt and THE ART
OF TYING THE CRAVAT (1828) by H. LeBlanc

LATE VICTORIAN WOMEN'S TAILORING by T. H. Holding

REGENCY ETIQUETTE: The Mirror of Graces
by A Lady of Distinction

SHIRTS AND MEN'S HABERDASHERY 1840s-1920s
by R. L. Shep and Gail Cariou

TAILORING OF THE BELLE EPOQUE: Vincent's Systems of
Cutting All Kinds of Tailor-Made Garments (1903)
by W. D. F. Vincent

VICTORIAN NEEDLE-CRAFT: Artistic & Practical (1889)

WOMEN'S COSTUME 1877-1885: The Complete Dress &
Cloak Cutter by Charles Hecklinger

For more information and prices, write to:

Fred Struthers, distributor

R. L. Shep Publications

Box 2706 • Fort Bragg, CA 95437 • USA

fsbks@mcn.org   www.rlshep.com

Titles published by R.L.Shep

ART IN DRESS (1922) by P. Clement Brown

ART OF CUTTING & HISTORY OF ENGLISH COSTUME
by Edward Giles

THE BOOK OF COSTUME or Annals of Fashion (1846)
by The Countess of Wilton

"THE BLUE BOOK OF MEN'S TAILORING"(1907)
by Frederick T. Croonborg

CIVIL WAR COOKING (1861):
The Housekeeper's Encyclopedia by Mrs. E. F. Haskell

CIVIL WAR ERA ETIQUETTE:
Martine's Handbook & Vulgarisms in Conversation

CIVIL WAR GENTLEMEN: 1860s Apparel Arts & Uniform

CIVIL WAR LADIES:
Fashions & Needle-Arts of the Early 1860s

COMPLETE GUIDE TO PRACTICAL CUTTING (1853)
by Edward Minister

CORSETS: A Visual History (mid 1800s - 1930s)

DRESS & CLOAK CUTTER (1877-1882)
by Charles Hecklinger

EARLY VICTORIAN MEN: The Tailor's Masterpiece,
All Kinds of Coats (1833) by George Walker

EDWARDIAN HATS: The Art of Millinery (1909)
by Mme. Anna Ben-Yusuf

EDWARDIAN LADIES TAILORING: 20th Century
System of Ladies' Garment Cutting (1910) by J. C. Hopkins

FEDERALIST AND REGENCY COSTUME: 1790-1819

FREAKS OF FASHION: The Corset & the Crinoline
by William Berry Lord

THE GREAT WAR: Styles and Patterns of the 1910s